DAD-
isms

**Also by Geoff Tibballs and
published by Michael O'Mara Books**

The Grumpy Old Git's Guide to Life

Crap Teams

The Seniors' Survival Guide: New Tricks for Old Dogs

Senior Jokes (The Ones You Can Remember)

*Seriously Senior Moments
(Or, Have You Bought This Book Before?)*

DAD-
isms

The Crazy Things
Dads Say and Do

GEOFF TIBBALLS

Michael O'Mara Books Limited

This paperback edition first published in 2023

First published in Great Britain in 2021 by
Michael O'Mara Books Limited
9 Lion Yard
Tremadoc Road
London SW4 7NQ

A CIP catalogue record for this book is available from the British Library.

This product is made of material from well-managed, FSC®-certified forests and other controlled sources. The manufacturing processes conform to the environmental regulations of the country of origin.

ISBN: 978-1-78929-518-4 in paperback print format
ISBN: 978-1-78929-301-2 in ebook format

1 2 3 4 5 6 7 8 9 10

Designed and typeset by D23
Illustrations by Andrew Pinder
Cover design by www.us-now.com
Cover illustration from shutterstock.com

Printed and bound by CPI Group (UK) Ltd, Croydon, CR0 4YY

www.mombooks.com

CONTENTS

CONTENTS

INTRODUCTION

Something changes when you become a dad. And it's not just the tangible things like being unable to remember the last time you had a good night's sleep, or accepting that actually your hair looks better when streaked with baby food, or even coming to the conclusion that a full nappy within an inch or two of your nose is, just maybe, not quite the worst smell in the world; you change as a person, too. You suddenly become *responsible*, forgoing a night out with your mates in favour of listening to a baby monitor for three, yes THREE, hours.

Almost overnight, the most precious bottle in your world is no longer Budweiser but formula milk. However, with this newfound responsibility can come a feeling that fatherhood is in danger of ageing you prematurely. So, just to demonstrate that you're still young at heart, you tend to over compensate with ill-advised dancing at family gatherings and by wearing shirts so loud you get sued by the Noise Abatement Society. In extreme cases, this desperation to recapture one's youth can even manifest itself in a ponytail.

Then, as your children grow older, you find that your once elevated, sophisticated, Augustan, even Wildean wit and sense of humour has been replaced by . . . dad jokes. To the dismay of your family, you realize that you have a ripe, corny joke for any occasion – and what's more, you are powerless to keep it to yourself. It's as if the moment you hear a feed line you are compelled to utter the same reply that everyone has heard countless times before. And they didn't laugh the first time, so they're certainly not going to start now. At best, you might get a kind of death rattle, self-garrotting groan; at worst, you could be sleeping on the sofa for three nights. But you are undeterred and, as sure as night follows day, you'll soon be bellowing out the same woeful cracks. It's an addiction. You can try medication, seek counselling, but there is no known cure for the prevention of telling Bad Dad Jokes. After all, as someone once said, a good pun is its own reword.

Even worse, imperceptibly, you find yourself turning into your own father, uttering those familiar dad-isms, some of which have been handed down from your great-great-great-great-GREAT grandaddy. And as your children become sharp, smart, upbeat teenagers you hear yourself doomed to repeat the very words your dad used when you were that age – complaining about today's fashion, why there's never anything decent on TV and why modern music is rubbish. Total, billowing RUBBISH. It's the circle of life. You don't need to rack your brains for new ways to embarrass teenage children – it comes naturally.

One of the most perceptive truisms about fatherhood is that nothing can ever prepare you for it. Not for having to read the same bedtime story every night for three years (AND twice on a Sunday); not for having managed to bribe your way to a rare, delicious moment of passion only to be interrupted by 'Dad, I need a drink of water. NOW!'; and nothing prepares you for having to learn simultaneous equations all over again to help with homework because somebody, somewhere, in the education system still thinks that they are actually relevant.

Yes, it can be tough being a dad, pretending you know what you're doing. So when we think back to all the times our dads gave us a lift home late at night because we had missed the last bus, lent us money when we most needed it (and at very reasonable interest rates) or offered smart advice on chat-up lines (even though we probably didn't appreciate it at the time), perhaps we can forgive them for their quirky sayings, embarrassing ways and absolutely dreadful jokes. Because without them, they wouldn't be proper dads. Would they?

● ●

'My dad still has this knack of embarrassing me. I have this dream that I'm at Buckingham Palace collecting my MBE from the Queen for being a smashing guy and he says: "Do you know he didn't have a proper girlfriend till he was nineteen?"'

GARY STRANG (MARTIN CLUNES),
MEN BEHAVING BADLY

● ●

QUESTIONS THAT EVERY DAD SHOULD ANSWER

- **Why do dads have to sneeze so loudly, adding a theatrical 'ATCHOO!' to a simple, regular sneeze?**

- Why would dads rather give up custody of their children than surrender custody of the TV remote?

- **Why do dads ask their children for such weird presents for their birthday, like antifreeze or six bags of multipurpose compost?**

- Why are dads so obsessed with cooking at barbecues when they only ever set foot in the kitchen to raid the fridge?

- **Why do dads play videos on their phone at full volume?**

- Why do dads say the full phone number (and so aggressively) when someone calls the home landline? How does the caller respond to THAT?

- **Why do dads think they know better than a GPS?**

- Why do dads spend fifteen minutes TV channel hopping? So when they do eventually find something everyone (after a humungous, volcanic row) agrees to watch, no one has a clue what's happening because they've missed the flipping start. And then they fall asleep.

- **Why do dads think it's amusing to fart in public?**

- Why do dads always have to tell you the precise road route they took to reach your house? Nobody cares.

- **Why do dads choose to eat any food that is left on other people's plates rather than throw it out, even if it gives them a glaring, triumphal rash. ('NO, we're NOT rubbing cream in it. Not THERE.')**

- Why do dads take it as a personal affront that that their children can text much faster than them?

- **Why do dads talk about their ingrowing purple toenail when giving a lift to their teenage offspring and the new boy/girlfriend?**

- Why do dads never read the instruction manual of a new appliance because 'It's easy, it's child's play,' and then complain bitterly when they can't get it to work?

- **Why do dads pretend that the train set they have bought is for their child when really it is for them?**

- Why do dads wolf down their food as if it's the first meal they've had for three months?

- **Why do dads quickly fall asleep in a comfy chair even though they're not really tired?**

- Why do dads put their young sons in such terrible fancy dress outfits? When all the other kids at the party are dressed as Batman or Superman, it's no use a dad protesting, 'It's all that was left in the shop,' when presenting a six-year-old son with the costume of a Japanese World War II naval commander.

- **Why do dads turn the car radio off when they are looking for a parking spot?**

- Why do dads prefer to drive around a car park for twenty minutes waiting for the perfect spot to appear rather than just park the car twenty feet further away?

- **Why do dads take enormous pride in squeezing their car into a tight parking spot, even though it means nobody can actually get out of the car?**

- Why do dads leave the bathroom door open while they are using the toilet?

- **And why do they pee so loudly that you have to plug your fingers in your ears?**

- Why do dads measure the quality of a hotel room not by the view or the space, but by the size and model of the TV?

- **Why is it that the first thing dads do when arriving in a foreign hotel room is check what channels the TV receives?**

- Why, if they have to sign a form in a store, do dads always prefer to use the cheap plastic ballpoint pen they brought with them rather than the expensive silver pen offered by the manager?

- **Why do dads shopping in a supermarket only ever want to buy cakes and cookies?**

- Why do dads lecture you about not drinking too much before you go out on a date, but on your way out of the door ask you to fetch them a beer from the fridge?

- **Why do dads think it is perfectly safe to eat food that is two months past its expiry date? Even when struck down with food poisoning, they blame it on anything except the yogurt that had started to turn green.**

- Why do dads give away the ending of a film you are watching just because they have seen it before?

- **Why do dads get so excited by the free mint bowl at a restaurant? It's as if they have won the lottery.**

- Why do dads think they are at least twenty years younger than they actually are?

- **Why do dads take their kids to the park or the beach to fly a kite, but the kids never get a go?**

- Why do dads feel the need to boast about the amount of packed, grey, fluffy lint that has collected in their belly button?

- **Why do dads always think they can sing?**

- Why do dads always think they are funny?

Daddy Cool?

To avoid the embarrassment of being seen with his dad by his classmates, fifteen-year-old Brooklyn Beckham used to tell David to drop him off before they got to school. Unfortunately David's mischievous sense of humour then took over. He told Jimmy Kimmel's US TV chat show in 2015: 'He (Brooklyn) tells me to park him around the corner. After doing it about five times on the trot, I'm driving around and he's just walking in his school, and I open the window and I said: "Brooklyn! I love you!" Obviously it didn't go down very well.

'With my middle son, Romeo, who's twelve, as soon as I take him into school, I'll go to kiss him and he'll turn his cheek. I will then pick him up and give him a bear hug and kiss him in front of his friends!' Maybe having David Beckham for a dad isn't so cool after all.

THE COMEBACK DAD
(a dad's quickfire wit knows no limits)

'Dad, put the kettle on.'
'If you think it'll suit me.'

'Dad, call me a taxi.'
'You're a taxi.'

'Dad, when are you coming round?'
'I haven't been unconscious.'

'Dad, do they serve prawns in this restaurant?'
'They'll serve anyone.'

'Dad, do you have a match?'
'Sure, your face and my arse!'

'Dad, make me a sandwich.'
'Abracadabra! You're a sandwich.'

'Dad, can you clear the table?'
'I'll try, but I might need to take a long run-up.'

* *

'Fathers don't wear bathing suits, they wear trunks.
It's kind of the same thing a tree would
wear if it went swimming.'

JERRY SEINFELD

* *

Get Home Now!

Halfway through a punk gig at a local pub, sixteen-year-old Jason's evening came to an abrupt end when his irate father marched in and dragged him home. What made it all the more embarrassing was that Jason was the band's singer.

EMBARRASSING THINGS DADS DO ON VACATION

- For at least a month in advance he takes an obsessive interest in the resort's weather forecast.

- **And for at least two months is obsessed by the exchange rate.**

- To allow for unscheduled breakdowns, roadworks, traffic jams and meteorite landings on the way to the airport, he devises a strict departure timetable for your 6am flight. This ensures the family checks in at least six hours before the plane takes off.

- **If driving to the destination, he insists on leaving the day before . . . and promptly runs into all the other dads who have had the same idea.**

- He belly flops into the hotel pool and has to apologize to everyone relaxing on the poolside area within a radius of fifty feet.

19

- **He gets sunburn so severe that waiters start addressing him as 'Mr Thermidor'.**

- He sucks in his stomach every time a pretty young woman walks past.

- **He insists on wearing socks with sandals.**

- He wears a T-shirt so tight that three people are needed to help him take it off.

- **He wears sunglasses everywhere to try to look cool, but is so unaccustomed to them he keeps walking into walls.**

- He tucks his shirt into his shorts.

- **He keeps checking on what the weather is like back home, and becomes irritated if it is good.**

- He forbids the family from using the hotel room minibar because of the exorbitant prices. 'If you need water, there's a perfectly good supermarket only forty-five minutes' walk away.'

- **At dinner he wears a Hawaiian shirt with a tie.**

- To display his linguistic skills, he tries to converse with the waitress in her native tongue but, instead of ordering another beer, he gets the wording slightly wrong and ends up trying to marry her mother.

- **He converses in Italian or Spanish simply by adding 'o' to the English word.**

- He piles his plate up so high at the hotel buffet that it starts to buckle under the weight.

- **He doesn't just go back for seconds, he goes back for thirds.**

- He fights little children for the last scoop of ice cream.

- **He refuses to let his children stroke any cat or dog in case the animal is rabid.**

- He snores so loudly in bed after a few drinks that you'd swear a pair of mating walruses were in the room.

- **He does dad dancing at the hotel disco.**

- He tries to show off by haggling with a market seller over the price of a 'genuine Rolex watch' and manages to obtain it at a fraction of its marked price. Unfortunately, the fraction is five-fourths.

. . . .

'What Dad means by "see", of course, is drive past at 67mph. Dad feels it is a foolish waste of valuable vacation time to get out of the car and actually go look at an attraction.'

DAVE BARRY

. . . .

DAD JOKES

Dad: I heard on the radio that a famous actress just killed someone.
Mum: Oh, who was it?
Dad: I can't remember. Is there an actress called Reese something?
Mum: Witherspoon?
Dad: No, it was with a knife.

Why aren't dogs good dancers?
Because they have two left feet.

When I was your age I hated facial hair, but then it started to grow on me.

Why did the man quit his job at a shoe recycling shop?
It was sole destroying.

I'm so good at sleeping I can do it with my eyes closed.

Why do bees have sticky hair?
Because they use a honeycomb.

I don't like funerals that start before noon. I guess I'm just not a mourning person.

What do you do with a wombat?
Play wom.

How many ears does Captain Kirk have?
Three: the left ear, the right ear and the final frontier.

What does the dentist of the year get?
A little plaque.

What's the difference between a train and a tree?
One leaves its shed and the other sheds its leaves.

I tried drag racing the other day, but it's really hard trying to run in heels.

How do you make antifreeze?

Steal her blanket.

That cemetery looks overcrowded.
People must be dying to get in there.

How is a bicycle like a duck?

Both have handlebars, except the duck.

How does Darth Vader like his toast?

On the dark side.

When your mum told me to stop acting like a
flamingo, I had to put my foot down.

What's orange and sounds like a parrot?

A carrot.

What do you get when you drop a piano on
an army base?

A Flat Major.

A woman was in court after pleading guilty to beating
her husband to death with his guitar collection.
'First offender?' asked the judge. 'No,' said her
lawyer. 'First a Gibson. Then a Fender.'

• •

'My father was never proud of me. One day he asked me, "How old are you?" I said, "I'm five." He said, "When I was your age, I was six."'

STEVEN WRIGHT

• •

A DAD'S GUIDE TO DAUGHTERS DATING

'You're wearing too much make-up.'

'I hope you're not going out dressed like that. You'll catch your death of cold.'

'That skirt's far too short. It's almost indecent. You'll give him the wrong idea.'

'What's this boy like? What's his name? I need to do a full background check on him.'

'He hasn't got piercings, has he? Or a Mohican?'

'Does he come from a good family?'

'Where does he live?'

'What are his job prospects?'

'You'll need a coat.'

'What team does he support?'

'Where is he taking you? Is alcohol served there?'

'Stick to Coca-Cola.'

**'Does this place have a phone number?
Don't worry, I'll look it up.'**

'How are you getting home? Do you want me to give you the number of a reputable taxi firm? I can come and meet you if you like.'

'If he so much as lays a finger on you I'll rip him to shreds.'

'Remember, back no later than eleven. Right? Right?'

'And no spending half an hour on the porch, because I'll be listening!'

'If any man tries to hurt you, tell them I have a gun, a shovel *and an alibi.*'

A DAD'S GUIDE TO SONS DATING

'Just go out and enjoy yourself. Don't do anything I wouldn't do.'

• •

'I will show him the same kind of respect that any father would show a forty-one-year-old man who dates his teenage daughter.'

AL BUNDY (ED O'NEILL), *MARRIED . . . WITH CHILDREN*

• •

Famous Dad

Vicky Cooper remembers how her dad, legendary comedy magician Tommy Cooper, loved nothing more than to make people laugh. On one occasion he complained to his long-suffering wife, Gwen, that he had indigestion. So she gave him a bottle of antacid medicine and he took some. As the liquid slipped down his throat, she told him: 'You're supposed to shake it first.' So he jumped up and down!

DADS AND THEIR CARS

A dad often sees his car as an extension of his personality. At one end of the scale you have the new, young, thrusting dad who drives a vehicle that is smooth, fast and sporty; at the other end you have the tired, careworn dad who drives something that rarely gets serviced, struggles when going uphill and regularly breaks down on family outings. One is state of the art; the other is state of the ark.

Of course, a car is also a status symbol, reflecting a family's success or lack of it. The dad with a new, expensive car will delight in showing off its advanced technology and features to friends and neighbours, even if they're not remotely interested. He actively yearns for a downpour just so that he can demonstrate the latest thing in windscreen wipers. Meanwhile, the dad with the old banger will tell people that it's just a runaround for the family and that his other car is a Porsche.

Whatever style of car a dad drives, the cleaning of it is all-important. The advent of automated car washes means that the weekly ritual of dads washing their cars manually on their driveways on a Sunday morning is not as common as it used to be, but with a little legwork you can still find the occasional telltale stream of soap and suds drifting into the roadside gutter. The dad who washes his car by hand takes enormous pride in the end result, spending hours washing, rinsing and polishing every inch of the bodywork until it positively gleams. Then, as he steps back to admire his handiwork, incontinent pigeons hover overhead. Thousands.

THINGS DADS ALWAYS SAY IN THE HOPE THAT ONE DAY SOMEONE WILL LAUGH

When someone falls over their feet,
a dad will always say:
'Did you enjoy your trip?'

**If a dad finds a small-denomination coin in the
street and gives it to his son or daughter,
he will always say:
'Don't spend it all at once.'**

If a dad sees another man washing his car or mowing
his lawn, he will always say:
'You can come and do mine when you've finished.'

**When a dad starts carving the Sunday roast
and a tiny slither of meat falls onto someone else's
empty plate, he will always say:
'Is that enough for you?'**

When a mum lifts a huge family pie out of the oven, the dad
always says, in front of everyone else:
'Oh, what are you all having?'

**When a dad encounters someone wearing
camouflage clothing, he will say he can't see him.**

In a stately home where the walls are lined with stuffed, mounted animal heads, a dad will always say:
'It must have been going fast when it hit that wall!'

When a cashier has trouble scanning an item, a dad will say:
'I guess it's free then.'

When eating mussels a dad will say:
'This one's too shy. It needs to come out of its shell.'

When he sees a promotion for an Iron Man contest, a dad will invariably say:
'I might enter that. I do all the ironing!'

When hearing police sirens, a dad will always say:
'They're coming for you.'

When watching a US TV cop show, a dad will say:
'That Officer Down guy is really unlucky. He gets shot almost every week.'

When playing cards, a dad will say:
'Here's a new game – fifty-two-card pickup. Do you want to play it?'
When the poor sod politely nods, the dad simply throws the entire deck of cards onto the floor and roars with laughter.

When driving past a field full of black and white
cows, a dad will say:
*'It must be cold out there because those
cows are Friesian!'*

**When the doorbell rings, a dad will ask one of his
children to answer it and will then add:
*'If it's the Invisible Man, tell him I can't see him!'***

In a bar a dad will suddenly turn to his wife or daughter
and say: *'You're beautiful. Your hair is lovely. Your skin is so soft.'*
She immediately looks at him and says: *'What's wrong with
you tonight? Stop being so daft.'* At which he
points to a bowl on the table and says:
'What do you mean? It's not me. It's the complimentary nuts!'

**When someone in the family announces that they
are just going out for a walk or to post a letter, but
come back seconds later because they have forgotten
something, a dad will always remark:
*'That was quick!'***

When out walking a dad will stop and say:
*'Hang on, I think I've got something in my shoe . . . Yes, I was right.
It's my foot.'* And then he will carry on walking, very pleased
with himself.

**When watching footballers go into a pre-match
huddle on TV, a dad will always remark:
*'Do you think they're talking about me?'***

**When the assistant in a grocery store asks him if he
wants the milk in a bag, a dad will joke:
*'No, I'd rather you left it in the carton.'***

Playing with spoonerisms, a dad will say
'I'm a fart smeller . . . I mean a smart feller.'
And he will think it's funny every time he says it.

**When a dad sees a house next to a cemetery,
he will not be able to resist saying:
*'At least the neighbours are quiet.'***

When a waiter asks him if he would like peas with his
meal, a dad will smile and say:
'Ah, no peas for the wicked.'

**When an insect gets splattered on the car
windscreen, a dad will say:
*'He won't have the guts to do that again.'***

33

YOU KNOW YOU'RE A DAD WHEN . . .

- **You start doing everything one-handed.**

- The sentence, 'Darling, could you take his foot out of my pocket?' sounds normal.

- **The vomit in which you are covered is not of your own making.**

- You come to realize that sleep is a luxury, not a necessity.

- **You genuinely prefer sleep to beer.**

- **You're afraid to say you're tired.**

- You are regularly used as a climbing frame.

- **You have started ten projects around the house and haven't finished one of them.**

- You struggle to name the members of the national football team but can identify every Care Bear.

- **The list of bodily fluids that disgust you has shortened to zero.**

- You spend forty-five minutes sweating, panting and groaning in the back seat of your car . . . trying to fix the new baby seat.

Presidential Quip

Even the coolest-ever President of the United States was not above making dad jokes. At the 2015 pre-Thanksgiving tradition of pardoning a turkey at the White House, Barack Obama, flanked by his daughters, Sasha and Malia, announced: 'This is my seventh year pardoning a turkey. Time flies . . .' before delivering the killer punchline, 'even if turkeys don't.' As the joke sank in and his daughters grimaced before laughing dutifully, he sought to excuse himself by adding: 'I thought it was pretty good.'

EMBARRASSING THINGS DADS DO AT WEDDINGS

- He reveals his daughter's childhood nickname in his father-of-the-bride speech.

- **He mentions all of her ex-boyfriends in his speech.**

- He does his Bugs Bunny impression during his speech. Nobody laughs.

- **His speech goes on for forty minutes. He ends it with a song.**

- At the formal wedding lunch he tries his trick of throwing an olive high into the air and catching it in his mouth.

- **He demands that the DJ at the reception puts on some proper music, like REO Speedwagon.**

- He loosens his tie and dances like someone trapped in a threshing machine.

- **After a few drinks he starts flirting with his daughter's new mother-in-law.**

- He asks his daughter's new husband in front of guests whether he wants any advice about birth control.

Day to Remember

Elaine from Dublin remembers how her dad made a big impact on her wedding day — but not necessarily for the right reason. It all started so well when he gave a really sweet speech that had everyone present in tears, but afterwards he got so drunk that he literally fell across a table in front of all her friends. 'I had to get my brothers to try to discreetly shuffle him up to his hotel room,' she said. 'If it wasn't for the fact that he had helped to pay for the wedding, I'd never have forgiven him.'

'Once my dad was drunk when my friend came over and he chased her around in a top hat, tailcoat and his underwear.'

KELLY OSBOURNE

DAD JOKES: THE SEQUEL

What has four wheels and flies?
A garbage truck.

What happened when the owl lost his voice?
He didn't give a hoot.

Why was the king only a foot tall?
Because he was a ruler.

Why did the can crusher quit his job?
It was soda-pressing.

What's pink and close to Silver?
The Lone Ranger's butt.

Why couldn't the bicycle stand up by itself?
It was two tyred.

I don't trust stairs. They're always up to something.

**What's the difference between
weather and climate?**
***You can't weather a tree but
you can climate.***

Did you hear about the baguette in the zoo?
It was bread in captivity.

Why do melons have weddings?
Because they cantaloupe.

Why did the tomato blush?
Because it saw the salad dressing.

How do you clean a tuba?
With a tuba toothpaste.

Short Shorts

Jason Hilley, from Orlando, Florida, was so horrified when his fourteen-year-old daughter, Kendall, purchased a pair of exceptionally short denim shorts that he decided to teach her a lesson about her fashion choices. He cut up an old pair of tight jean shorts, rolled them up and squeezed his frame into them. Confronting her, he vowed: 'You wear yours out in public, I will wear mine!' He also threatened to pick her up from school every day wearing them. Through tears of laughter, Kendall protested: 'These aren't even that short.' To which her dad replied: 'Nooo, neither are mine!' It was an argument she was never going to win.

Why did Sherlock Holmes's house have a yellow front door?
It was a lemon entry, my dear Watson.

My wife says she's leaving me because I'm totally obsessed with astronomy. What planet is she on?!

Why do nurses need red crayons?
Because sometimes they have to draw blood.

Why did the man fall down the well?
Because he couldn't see that well.

Sundays are always a little sad, but the day before is a sadder day.

My wife keeps telling me to stop pretending to be butter. But I'm on a roll now.

What's blue and smells like red paint?
Blue paint.

A DAD'S CRIES OF DESPAIR

'Has anyone seen my other sock?'

'Do you think I'm made of money?'

'Money doesn't grow on trees, you know.'

'Were you raised in a barn?'

'Do you ever look up from that phone?'

'Who left the tap running?'

'Who forgot to wipe their feet?'

'Who's brought mud into the house?'

'This is not a hotel, you know!'

'Do you think I run a taxi service?'

'Who's eaten the last biscuit?'

'Who put the marmalade knife in the butter?'

'Did anyone see where I put my glasses?'

'How much?!'
(When he hears the price of anything costing over five quid.)

'Whose wet towel is this?'

'How much longer are you going to be in the bathroom?'

**'Why is the central heating on?
If you're cold, put on a sweater.'**

'Who used all the hot water?'

• •

Antony Royle (Ralf Little): Dad, where were you
when Kennedy was killed?
Jim Royle (Ricky Tomlinson): What? Kennedy's dead?
Antony Royle: Well, you know they say everybody remembers
where they were when they heard he was killed?
Jim Royle: Well, I don't remember, but I bet our bloody
immersion heater was on!

THE ROYLE FAMILY

• •

A DAD'S GUIDE TO DIY

When it comes to home improvement, the key thing for any son or daughter to remember is that Dad knows best. He is in charge. He is the one with a toolbox filled with bent screwdrivers, rusty nails dating back to the 1970s, the national collection of broken wall plugs in a range of four different colours and odd leftover screws, of every shape and size, that he has refused to throw away over the years because you never know when they might come in useful.

This is his domain. His reason for being. What makes him a Real Dad. So he won't thank you for pointing out that the shelf he has just put up amid great fanfare is not straight. Questioning his eyesight is not an option, even though you can hardly forget that this was the man who cut your fringe when you were six, an incident from which you still bear the emotional scars. Still, you know you won't have to worry about the shelf for long because the chances are that the moment anyone places something on it the shelf will crash down. At which point your dad, refusing to take the blame for his shoddy workmanship, will rage: 'Who put that on my shelf? You're not supposed to put things on it!'

A DAD'S GUIDE TO PAINTING AND DECORATING

As a rule, a dad hates decorating. It is a time-consuming chore that takes him away from doing something more pleasurable like watching TV or sitting in the garden with a beer, and since it is his wife who has usually chosen the colour scheme, it typically means covering white walls and ceilings with another coat of white or, if she is feeling particularly carefree and expressive, magnolia. In short, painting the house is boring.

Should she suggest that instead of driving himself to distraction he should hire a professional decorator, he will instantly bristle: 'I'm not paying a load of money to get someone else to do a bit of painting. Have you seen what they charge?' Besides, employing a professional is an affront to his dignity, a slight on his artistic ability. No, he will go ahead and paint the lounge, but he will never miss the opportunity to let everyone know that he is doing it under sufferance. In terms of martyrdom, Joan of Arc had nothing on a determined dad with a paint roller.

Then the moaning starts. 'The paint's too runny.' 'The roller is useless.' 'The brushes keep moulting.' 'The paint is splattering my face.' Nothing is right. And it's even worse if he's hanging wallpaper, when a dreaded bubble will inevitably appear at the most inaccessible point. This requires dragging the wallpaper off the wall, often in a fit of pique that risks causing a tear, and then beating the bubble into submission with a soft brush. When the wallpaper is finally flat, he steps back only to see that he has been so brutal with his extermination of the bubble that the

43

wallpaper design is no longer lined up with the adjacent strip. This realization is followed by the familiar paternal cry: 'I said we should have PAINTED it!'

This drama can go on for several days. At the end, when he is at last in a position to call you in to admire his handiwork, you must be positive and complimentary, bearing in mind the suffering that he – and the rest of the family – has been through all week. You are tempted to say, 'Dad, you've missed a bit,' but don't. Please. Never. Not worth it.

THINGS YOU MIGHT HEAR WHILE YOUR DAD IS DOING DIY

'There's something wrong with these walls.'

'These nails are useless.'

'This hammer is useless.'

'This chisel is useless.'

'Why don't screws ever go in straight?'

'Why don't things ever fit properly?'

'Well, you have a go if you think you can do better.'

'Why don't they make paint like they used to? I'm sure they deliberately thin it down these days to save money.'

'There's more paint on me than there is on the wall!'

'This is the last time I'm decorating.'

• •

'Sometimes I am amazed that my wife and I created two human beings from scratch, yet struggle to assemble the most basic of IKEA cabinets.'

GREG KINNEAR

• •

THE COMEBACK DAD

'Dad, why did you trace your family tree?'
'Because I'm not very good at drawing freehand.'

'Dad, I feel like a Danish pastry.'
'That's odd. You don't look like one.'

'Dad, I'm off.'
'I wondered what the smell was.'

'Dad, say something funny.'
'Something funny.'

'Dad, where did the Romans keep their armies?'
'Up their sleevies.'

'Dad, what time is it?'
'Time you got a watch.'

'Dad, I'm just going to file my nails.'
'Under what?'

**'Dad, I can't do my maths homework.
If I had nineteen cookies and ate twelve,
what would I get?'**
'Indigestion.'

. . . .

'My dad used to say: "Keep your chin up, son." He once broke his
jaw walking into a lamp post.'

ADAM SANDLER

. . . .

Celebrity Crush

When Anais Gallagher was fourteen, rock-star dad Noel
seriously embarrassed her in front of One Direction's
Harry Styles. Anais was a big fan of One Direction and
had made the mistake of telling her dad that she would
probably wet herself if the band walked into the café where
they were sitting. So when, as if by magic, Styles appeared,
Noel started kicking her under the table and shouted in his
inimitable style: 'Are you going to wet yourself now?' Anais
said: 'I literally died!' (Editor's note: she didn't.)

ESSENTIAL DAD PHRASES

'When I was your age . . .'

'He's as thick as two short planks.'

'I wasn't asleep. I was just resting my eyes.'

'They don't make them like they used to.'

'What time do you call this?'

'Don't look at me in that tone of voice.'

'I can remember when all this was fields.'

'Ah, those were the days.'

'Wait till you have children of your own.'

'Who said life was fair?'

'Act your age.'

'My father used to tell me . . .'

'Don't forget, I was young once.'

'Is it warm/stifling/cold/draughty in here, or is it just me?'

'I only stopped off for one quick drink.'

'You'll have someone's eye out with that.'

'You certainly didn't get that from me.'

(If their child asks for a puppy) 'You do know you'll have to walk it?'

'If someone told you to jump off a cliff, would you do it?'

(When receiving the bill in a restaurant) 'What's the damage?'

'It's not a tear. There's something in my eye.'

'It's character-building.'

(On your birthday) 'Well, does it feel any different?'

(On his birthday) 'Now don't go spending a lot on me.'

'Eat it. It will put hairs on your chest.'

'You're only young once.'

**'If you fall and break a leg, don't come
running to me.'**

'Don't let the bedbugs bite.'

'Ask your mother.'

Grandad's Teeth

Althia Davis, from Victoria, Australia, remembers the time she was waiting in a shop with her father and her five-year-old son, who was taking a keen interest in a bowl of lollipops on the counter. So when the man behind the counter asked the boy if he would like one, he quickly said, 'Yes, please.' The man also asked Althia's dad if he wanted a lollipop, but before he could answer, the boy said: 'Oh no, you can't give Grandad any because he hasn't got any teeth.' Hearing this, Althia's father replied: 'Oh yes I have! They're in my pocket.' And he proceeded to take them out and fit them in his mouth – just so that he could have a lollipop.

• •

'Don't bring home one of those young ones, Dad –
no one younger than me, please.'

JADE JAGGER, CONCERNED ABOUT DAD MICK'S DATING PLANS

• •

Bathroom Etiquette

All dads have their stock sayings. Jay says that whenever he used to tell his dad that he was going to the bathroom, his dad would reply: 'Mention my name and you'll get a good seat.'

DADS AND THEIR GADGETS

Dads do love their toys and if the children are too busy to let him play with theirs, he has to play with toys of his own. These usually take the form of novelty items designed to make his life simpler and his wallet lighter. For example, he can invest in . . .

- A device that ensures every pint of beer he drinks has a perfect head.

- **A robot lawnmower to achieve those perfect lines without leaving his chair.**

- A motion-activated toilet bowl light that glows whenever he enters the bathroom at night and therefore helps him improve his aim.

- **An eye-massager that enables him to relax after a long, tiring day.**

- A shower head with a built-in wireless speaker to provide backing vocals while he is singing in the shower.

Whatever gadget dad has acquired, he will instantly be filled with Mr Toad-like enthusiasm for it, proclaiming it to be the best thing since sliced bread. Naturally, he will insist on demonstrating its capabilities to everyone he meets. Even Jehovah's Witnesses are likely to be invited in to witness his latest toy in action. Alas, the novelty soon wears off and it dawns on him that his life-changing gadget is a total waste of money. Before long, it ends up hidden away in a corner of the garage next to his Segway, virtual drum kit and six pedometers.

GADGETS THAT EVERY DAD NEEDS

- A missing sock detector.

- **An app that tells him whenever his daughter is locking lips with a stranger.**

- An app that tells him when his partner is listening.

- **An automatic device for putting slippers on his feet.**

- An invisibility cloak so that the children leave him in peace at weekends.

- **An app that turns every traffic light green when he is late on the school run.**

- An ejector seat for when his children misbehave in the car on family outings.

- **A time machine so that he could travel back ten years and appreciate how difficult fatherhood was going to be before taking it on.**

- A device that automatically closes every door in the house when his children have left them open.

- **A device that automatically switches off every light in the house when his children have left them on.**

- An app that laughs at his jokes – no matter how bad they are.

TRUISMS

- Dad thinks he wears the trousers in the house, but it's always Mum who tells him which pair to put on.

- **There are three ways to get something done: do it yourself, hire someone or forbid your kids to do it.**

- Whoever proclaimed that a cat scratching its claws down a blackboard was the worst sound ever had obviously never heard a dad on karaoke night.

- **Hell hath no fury like a dad whose tools are mixed up.**

- Obtain one large, unhappy, live octopus. Stuff into a small net bag, making sure that all the arms stay inside. Congratulations, you have passed the baby-dressing test.

- **The only musical instrument most dads should be allowed near is the air guitar.**

- A bathroom is a place where your child doesn't need to go until you're backing your car out of the driveway.

- **A child in bed instinctively knows when visitors are in the lounge because it is the only time when Mum laughs at Dad's jokes.**

- Telling a teenager the facts of life is like giving a fish a bath.

- **There's nothing wrong with teenagers that reasoning with them won't aggravate.**

- For a dad, it's difficult to decide whether growing pains are something teenagers have – or are.

- **Home is a place where teenagers go to refuel.**

- Adolescence is a time of rapid change. Between the ages of twelve and seventeen, for example, a parent can age as much as twenty years.

- **The best time to give advice to your children is while they're still young enough to believe that you know what you're talking about.**

- Every father should remember that one day his son will follow his example and not his advice.

. . . .

'When I was a child and I'd fall over and cut myself,
I'd come staggering in from the backyard sobbing, snot
dripping down my top lip and my dad would look at
the blood on my knee or elbow and shout to my mum:
"Deirdre, go and get the saw out of the shed, I'll have to cut
it off," and then I'd start wailing like a banshee.'

PETER KAY, *THE SOUND OF LAUGHTER*

. . . .

A Load of Bull

Ruth and her parents were enjoying a pleasant afternoon walk in the countryside when they came across a field of cows. Her dad was wearing a bright red waterproof jacket (standard attire for a summer's day), but on a whim he suddenly decided to remove it and wave it at the cows as if he were a proud Spanish matador. His posturing went on for a couple of minutes, with ever more extravagant flourishes of his red 'cape', each one greeted by the cows' total disinterest. Just then Ruth heard a heavy pounding sound in the distance and glanced around to see a huge bull at the top of the field, heading straight for them at speed.

'Bull! Bull!' she shouted, running with her mother towards the gate. 'Dad, there's a bull! Get out!'

'Yeah, sure,' he replied, determined not to fall for such an obvious trick. But then he, too, heard the rumbling noise getting ever nearer and, to his horror, saw the bull. The snorting beast was now bounding down the hill at full throttle. The cows scattered and, in the nick of time, so did Ruth's dad, discarding his red jacket and vaulting over the gate to safety with seconds to spare. It had been a close shave, however, and he needed to buy a new pair of jeans the next day because he had torn them on the gate. He also needed to buy a new pair of underpants – for different reasons.

EMBARRASSING THINGS A DAD DOES ON SOCIAL MEDIA

- He posts forty-eight pictures of his daughter's second birthday party online.

- **He posts unflattering photos online of his teenage children without permission.**

- He posts photos part way through a family holiday in Spain, and returns home to find the house has been burgled.

- **He repeatedly tries to add his son as a friend on 'the Face Book', even though the son politely declines the offer every time.**

- He discovers that after eighteen months he still has only two Twitter followers – and one of those is his wife who likes to keep an eye on what he posts in case he gets into trouble.

- **He posts videos of himself dancing in the belief that it constitutes family entertainment.**

- He posts videos of himself singing along enthusiastically to Bon Jovi in the belief that it constitutes family entertainment.

- **He posts videos of himself wearing crazy clothes and pulling silly faces in the belief that it constitutes family entertainment.**

- He gets seriously trolled for his dancing, singing, crazy clothes and silly faces. And then he closes his account.

The Daughter Called Banana Face . . . Not

When Richard Holmes, from Birmingham, England, joked to his seven-year-old daughter, Katie-Ann, that her middle name was Banana Face, he never expected her to believe him . . . until nearly a month later when he read her school essay titled 'About Me'. For then it became clear that Katie-Ann had swallowed every word. She wrote: 'My middle name is very embarrassing. My middle name is Banana Face. I asked my mum and my dad and it was all because of my dad. I don't know why he gave me this middle name. I think it's wierd [sic] so I am going to keep it a secret to anyone who asks because they're going to laugh at me if I ever tell them. But I will never tell them even if they ask nicely.'

After reading the homework, her dad confessed and the pair burst out laughing. He said later: 'I told her that her middle name was Banana Face, because it was the first thing that came into my head. The way she reacted I just had to carry on the joke. I didn't think she believed me then and because I didn't hear anything else, I forgot about it. That was until I opened her homework. I was halfway through it and just started howling hysterically. So I told her it was a joke and there were tears coming down our faces. I don't think I'd ever seen her laugh that hard in my life.'

Surprise Visit

Coldplay singer Chris Martin was so proud when his sixteen-year-old daughter, Apple, landed her first job in a clothing store that he decided to pay a surprise visit to her workplace. 'I just went to see,' he said, 'and I thought, "I'd better buy something." So I took a T-shirt from the rack and lined up in the queue. She was at the checkout, and there were two checkouts, and she saw me and mouthed: "Dad, get out!" I felt terrible, so I moved to the other line.'

THINGS THAT DADS WILL EXCUSE FROM THE KIDS BUT MUMS WON'T

- An untidy bedroom.

- **Having an ice cream shortly before dinner.**

- Not eating all their vegetables at dinner.

- **Disturbing the neighbours.**

- Watching TV past their bedtime.

School Play

When Eric was six he was chosen to play third shepherd in his school's Christmas nativity play. He only had one line – 'Fetch some straw' – but his dad could not have been prouder. After all, as he told Eric, Meryl Streep started out by playing a donkey in a school play and Leonardo DiCaprio was once cast as 'pirate in background' in a school production of *Peter Pan*. (His dad made all this up for effect.) Anyway, the gist of the conversation was that if Eric made a good impression on stage, who knew where it could lead eventually . . . the West End . . . Hollywood . . . the Civic Theatre, Rotherham.

Come the night of the school play and the audience was full of anxious parents, all praying that their child would not freeze on stage. Eric's dad was so tense he was in danger of snapping in half. He knew when Eric's line was coming up and could hardly bear to watch. So, when Eric delivered the three words impeccably, the relief was so palpable that his dad, without thinking, leaped to his feet and started applauding feverishly, adding a few whistles of delight for good measure, forgetting that this was St Stephen's Junior School and not the Hollywood Bowl. All he succeeded in doing was embarrassing Eric, drowning out the rest of the scene and infuriating the other parents.

The head teacher firmly told him to sit down and be quiet or leave, and afterwards Eric had to explain sheepishly to his friends that the idiot in the audience was his dad.

- Rushing their breakfast.

- **Eating too many sweet treats (so long as they share them with Dad).**

- Forgetting to put the toilet seat down.

- **Talking with their mouth full (but only because Dad does it all the time).**

- Their teenage son getting drunk.

A Cure for Laziness

When his teenage son took a nap one Saturday afternoon, Essex dad Ben Jerome decided to teach him a lesson for being lazy. So after a while he went into the boy's room, woke him and said he needed to hurry up. 'I think you're going to be late for school,' Ben said, 'but you'll be all right, yeah?' As the bleary-eyed boy looked confused, he continued: 'It's Monday morning. You slept all the way through.'

As his son tried to process what was happening, Ben assured him that the noise downstairs was his siblings having breakfast before setting off for school. With the boy on the verge of tears, Ben could keep up the pretence no longer and confessed that it was still only Saturday afternoon. His son was none too impressed but Ben reckoned he would thank him for it later in life. In fact, even by Monday all had been forgiven.

SON AND DAD TEXT EXCHANGE

Son: 'I'm going to a party.'

Dad: 'Will you be drinking?'

Son: 'No.'

Dad: 'Will you be doing drugs?'

Son: 'No.'

Dad: 'Will you be having sex?'

Son: 'No.'

Dad: 'Then why the hell are you going?!'

DAD JOKES: THE SEQUEL TO THE SEQUEL

What did the left eye say to the right eye?
Between you and me, something smells.

My friend has designed an invisible airplane,
but I can't see it taking off.

What has two butts and kills people?
An assassin.

I'm reading a horror story in Braille.
Something bad is going to happen, I can just feel it.

**Why can't you hear a pterodactyl
go to the bathroom?**
Because the 'p' is silent.

What's the difference between an angry circus
owner and a Roman barber?
One is a raving showman, the other is a shaving Roman.

**My three favourite things are eating my family
and not using commas.**

What do you call a group of rabbits walking backwards?
A receding hare-line.

**I used to run a dating service for chickens, but I was
struggling to make hens meet.**

What is brown and not very heavy?
Light brown.

**Guess who I bumped into on my way to
get my glasses fixed?**
Everybody.

What did the father buffalo say to the boy buffalo
when he went to school?
Bison.

**My dad always told me to make the little things
count, so now I'm teaching maths to mice.**

How did the police come to arrest the paint thief?
They caught him red-handed.

What do you call a cow during an earthquake?
A milkshake.

The recipe said, 'Set the oven to 180 degrees.' But now I can't
open it because the door faces the wall.

Can a kangaroo jump higher than a house?
Of course. Houses can't jump.

What do you call the boss at Old McDonald's Farm?
The CIEIO.

The guy who stole my diary just died.
My thoughts are with his family.

What do you call a man who tells dad jokes
but isn't actually a dad?
A faux pa.

Shopping Errand

Alan's dad had rarely set foot inside a supermarket, but when his wife was ill one week she asked him to fetch some urgent shopping for her. Knowing that he might find this quite a challenge, she carefully wrote out a list of the items she needed, and numbered them from one to six to make it simpler for him to understand. An hour later he returned with four huge bags of shopping and proudly announced that he had ticked off every item on the list. As he unpacked the bags, she saw to her horror that he had bought one banana, two joints of beef, three potatoes, four bags of flour, five dozen eggs and six multipacks of toilet rolls.

A DAD'S GUIDE TO DRIVING LESSONS

There will probably come a time in life when your dad will offer to give you driving lessons, partly to save money but also because he thinks you need to learn from the best. And all dads see themselves as excellent drivers. Forget about the occasional speeding ticket ('Why don't the police target real criminals?'), the mild road rage ('Why are there so many idiots on the road?') and the time he drove into a lamp post ('What a stupid place to put a lamp post!') – any mishaps are always somebody else's

fault. However, good drivers do not necessarily make good teachers, as you will quickly discover.

If it's not daunting enough sitting behind the wheel of your dad's car, knowing that any tiny scratch or scrape on the precious bodywork will give him sleepless nights, there is the distinct feeling that he is even more nervous about the experience than you are. He is desperately trying to appear calm and unruffled, but there is something in the way he suddenly yells things like 'Watch out for that parked car!', 'Mind that old lady!' and 'Brake! Brake now! NOW!' that hints at an underlying anxiety. Be prepared for him to grab the steering wheel when you least expect it or, following a particularly stressful lesson, to find him looking up the price of an ejector seat.

A DAD'S GUIDE TO CAR BUYING

If you do manage to pass your test – either thanks to, or in spite of, your dad – his next involvement will come with the buying of a car. Forget any notion about going by yourself to a dealer and simply purchasing the second-hand car of your choice, your dad will insist on accompanying and advising you every single step of the way.

Casting his expert eye over the vehicles on display, he will steer you away from the sporty model you liked the look of in favour of a staid family saloon. Consequently, instead of a sleek convertible with rapid acceleration and surround sound, your first car ends up being something that goes from nought to sixty in about five minutes, has a seventies radio and is usually driven by pensioners in cardigans. But, as your dad points out, it is solid and reliable and the roof rack may come in useful one day. Worse still, you know in your heart of hearts that he's probably right.

A DAD'S GUIDE TO VEHICLE MAINTENANCE

Dads trust garages only marginally more than they trust politicians. They are convinced – and often with justification – that the mechanics don't know what they're doing and that bogus faults are invented to bump up the bill. You can take a car in with a leaky carburettor and end up having to pay for a whole new engine, new tyres and ten brake pads. According to the garage, even the back window furry dice were dangerously worn and needed replacing.

To illustrate what he considers to be sharp practice, your dad will complain along the lines of: 'How often do you go to hospital with a broken arm and find that six more bones are broken while you're in there?' So he prides himself on being able to carry out *any* vehicle repairs. And he is never happier than when he is wearing his old overalls, spanner in hand, up to his elbows in grease, staring at an engine for hours and hours. The more parts that he can dismantle and then replace, the happier he is. If that means the kitchen floor being littered with car engine components while the family is trying to eat lunch, so be it. And if his labours actually result in the car starting again, his day, his week, his *month* is made. Just be prepared for having to listen to a blow by blow account of how he did it. Every . . . single . . . day.

THINGS YOUR DAD WILL SAY BEFORE YOUR FIRST SOLO DRIVE

'Have you checked your oil?'

'Do you know how the windscreen wipers work?'

'Have you got your phone with you?'

'Remember to look out for cyclists . . . and pedestrians who suddenly wander into the road . . . and learner drivers . . . and buses that pull out without indicating.'

'Remember there are roadworks on Queen Street.'

'Avoid that hill by the church in case you stall halfway up. You know you're not good with hill starts.'

'Are you sure you don't want me to come with you?'

'Call me when you get there.'

'Have you listed me or your mother as next of kin?'

Revenge at Last

The day after passing his test, Kieran was eager to take his dad out in the car for the first time as a qualified driver. 'Sure,' said his dad. But to Kieran's surprise, his dad jumped into the back behind the driver's seat. 'Why aren't you sitting in the passenger seat?' asked Kieran. 'Son,' said the dad with a grin, 'I've been waiting for this moment since you were a small boy. Now it's my turn to sit back here and kick the seat while you try to concentrate on driving!'

THE WORLD ACCORDING TO DAD

'Swearing is caring.'

'Blood is thicker than water, and much more difficult to get out of the carpet.'

'Essential oils are used to fry chicken wings, onion rings or French fries. All other oils are NOT essential.'

'The only substitute for good manners is fast reflexes.'

**'A chip on the shoulder is an indication
of wood higher up.'**

'The best way to serve cabbage is to someone else.'

**'There are better things in life than alcohol, but
alcohol makes up for not having them.'**

'How long a minute is depends on which side of the
bathroom door you're on.'

'A bird in the hand makes blowing your nose difficult.'

'Every snowflake in an avalanche pleads not guilty.'

'Work is for people who don't know how to fish.'

'He who laughs last, thinks slowest.

**'A clear conscience is usually the sign
of a bad memory.'**

'The road to success is always under construction.'

**'Time may be a great healer, but it's
a lousy beautician.'**

'Life is like a sewer. What you get out of it depends
on what you put into it.'

Lost in Translation

As part of her university languages course, Susanna spent four months in Austria teaching English at a German-speaking school. Her parents flew out from England to visit her and to embrace the local culture, even though her dad's knowledge of the German language was pretty much limited to *'ein, zwei, drei'*, *'Verboten'*, *'Sprechen Sie Englisch?'* and a couple of other words picked up from war films. However, this was not really a problem when they all ate out together because Susanna was fluent in German and was more than happy to do the talking.

One evening the three of them dined at a local Japanese restaurant. At the end of the meal, Susanna's dad produced his credit card to indicate that he was ready to pay. The waitress came over and asked, *'Zusammen?'*, which is German for 'together', i.e. checking whether he was going to pay for all three meals. However, being unfamiliar with the word, he thought the waitress was speaking English and had said, 'Two salmon?', so he helpfully replied, 'No, I had chicken.' The waitress glared at him blankly until Susanna, gamely stifling her laughter, spoke to her in German along the lines of, 'Please excuse my dad. He's an idiot.' After that, he agreed to learn a few more German words, but until then to leave all communication to his daughter.

DADS AND THEIR SHEDS

If a dad suddenly disappears unannounced and nobody knows where he is, unless the toilet seat can be heard straining under his weight, there is a strong chance that he is in his garden shed. This is his hiding place of choice, the tranquil refuge where he is able to escape from the hurly-burly of a house full of boisterous children. It has the added bonus of putting him out of earshot, with the perfect excuse for not responding to cries of, 'Tidy up the lounge, NOW!' This means that long after his children have grown up and left home, a dad will (out of habit) still quietly retire to his shed for a couple of hours of MQT (mega quiet time).

What he does in there is a mystery to the outside world. There may be some evidence of industry although the fact that his lovingly crafted, handmade wooden kitchen stool remains unfinished after twenty-seven years suggests that the pace of work is leisurely. He may leave a saw or a plane lying around to imply that progress is being made, but these are just diversions to disguise the fact that he uses his shed for little more than contemplation and to dream of things that make him truly content – like sun-kissed beaches, Elle Macpherson, the Ferrari 488 Pista and, perhaps most of all, doughnuts.

• •

'When the kids have their friends round, I have to pretend
to be Fun Dad so they won't go back to their parents and say:
"He was really shouty."'

JONATHAN ROSS

• •

A Voice from the Coffin

Shay Bradley left his family and other mourners in stitches
with a message from beyond the grave. As his coffin was
being lowered into the ground at his 2019 funeral in Kilkenny,
Ireland, his voice was suddenly heard calling: 'Hello? Hello?
Let me out! Where am I? Let me out! It's dark in here! Is
that the priest I can hear? This is Shay. I'm in the box. No,
in front of you!'

He had been ill for a long time and had made the audio
recording about a year before his death. His daughter,
Andrea, who knew about the message, said: 'It was his way
of saying, "OK, the sadness is over now – here is a laugh so
you can go and celebrate my life with a smile on your face."
He would love to know how many people he made laugh
with it. He was an amazing character.'

HE WHO MUST BE OBEYED

Dads aren't always very adept at disciplining their children. It doesn't come naturally to them. They'd much rather be releasing their inner child by having fun with their kids and leave the hard yards to the mum. But sometimes their frustration boils over and, if only to show their partner that they are not willing to let the kids totally run riot, dads will resort to the following phrases from the paternal handbook:

'Do I look stupid?' (This is strictly rhetorical)

'What part of "no" don't you understand?'

'While you're under my roof, you'll do as I say.'

'Wait until I get you home!'

'When you pay the mortgage, you can make the rules.'

'Am I talking to a brick wall?'

'If I've told you once, I've told you a thousand times.'

'I'm not going to tell you again.'

'I'm not yelling at you. I'm helping you hear.'

'I don't care what other people are doing. I'm not everybody else's father!'

**'I'm not talking just to hear the sound of
my own voice.'**

'You're going to like it, whether you like it or not!'

**'If you don't stop crying, I'll give you something
to cry about.'**

'What's so funny? Wipe that
smile off your face.'

'Why? Because I said so.'

● ●

Peter Griffin: I've had a good life. And you can always be
proud of your father and all of his accomplishments.
Meg Griffin: What accomplishments?
Peter Griffin: Go to your room.

FAMILY GUY

● ●

THINGS DADS DO BUT REALLY SHOULDN'T

- Take photos of their children when they are teenagers. Dads love to take endless photos and videos of their children when they are young and it's rarely a problem then, but once kids turn into teenagers they become more camera shy than the average bank robber. Yet still dads persist with the camera, which usually results in hands over eyes, sulky faces or jackets pulled up over heads. The overall effect is less a happy family snap and more the look of someone being dragged into court.

- Try to be best friends with their children. Some parenting guides might list this as a goal but it rarely works in practice. The only teenagers who want to hang out with their dads all the time are ones who have no friends of their own age – and that's probably because their dad is always around. Anyway, isn't there an unwritten rule about never asking a friend for money? So that rules dad out as a friend straight away.

- Give their children pet names and then use them in public because no eleven-year-old wants to have to explain to their friends why their dad calls them 'Petal', especially when their real name is Kevin.

- Try to impress their children by being the life and soul of every party. Most children would prefer their dad to be invisible in public instead of being the one who always volunteers to run the school disco. And why do dads upstage their twelfth birthday party with an impromptu display of Greek dancing, or willingly dress up as a buxom barmaid for charity.

- Compare their children to their siblings or cousins. 'Why can't you be more like Michael?' Dad will say. 'He's such a popular boy, with lots of friends, he got wonderful school reports and was always top of his class.' To which their son will reply: 'Dad, I'm fifty-seven. It's my life. Deal with it.'

- Take their children on character-building country walks when they would be much happier at home playing video games. Besides, how many youngsters want to risk their friends seeing them in a woolly hat, kagoule and hiking boots?

- Mimic their children when they whine. Dads may think that copying their daughter's plaintive cry of 'I don't want to wear the pink dress' is funny but all it does is blur the lines as to who is the grown-up. Anyway, the pink dress is awful. And dad should know. He chose it in the shop, which is why he is making such a big deal about it. By rejecting it, not only is she showing a lack of gratitude, she is daring to question his fashion taste. So wise and she's still only four.

- Comment every time they break wind, saying things like, 'I needed that', 'That one came out with its boots on', 'It must be that chicken dinner', 'Don't strike a match near me' or 'That's better out than in.'

- Break wind and blame it on the cat.

- Change TV channels at the first hint of anything unsuitable on the screen. Even if it is just two insects copulating in a wildlife programme, some dads will grab the remote and say: 'I don't think we want to see any more of that sort of thing.'

- Rap along to a rap song whenever they hear one on the radio. This usually amounts to going, 'Yo, yo, yo.'

- Lick the lid of the ice-cream tub when it is empty.

- Spend hours wondering what the one thing is that Meat Loaf won't do for love.

- Describe in graphic detail the poo they have just done, followed by the familiar warning: 'I wouldn't go in there for a while if I were you.'

- Automatically assume that their teenage daughter's new boyfriend is, at the very least, an axe murderer.

Welcome Surprise

Every time graduate student Courtney Payne flies back to her Missouri home from her university in Portland, Oregon, she knows that dad Doug will be waiting for her at Kansas City International Airport. What she doesn't know is what new way he has devised to embarrass her in public.

It all started in November 2018 when Doug decided to meet her at Arrivals holding up a card that read 'Kardashian'. Doug said: 'People would ask me, "Is it really the Kardashians?" And I'll say, "Yeah, it's Daniel Kardashian," or somebody who's not even a Kardashian.' Buoyed by that success, Doug has since welcomed his daughter home with cards reading 'Miss Oregon' (technically correct because she was single and had arrived from Oregon) and country singer Miranda Lambert.

In December 2019, he went further still by donning a full green elf costume and holding a sign that read 'Santa's Naughty List' with Courtney's name written below. 'When they first saw me as an elf, some people at the airport probably thought I was a deranged individual,' admitted Doug, 'but once they saw the sign and realized what I was doing, it put a smile on their face.'

- Take an unhealthy interest in their children's love lives. The interrogation can be relentless. 'Are you seeing anyone?' 'Why aren't you seeing anyone?' 'Are you seeing anyone special?' 'Why aren't you seeing so-and-so anymore?' 'Are you taking precautions?' 'When are you going to settle down?' 'Have you thought about moving into a place of your own?' 'When are you going to give your mother and I the grandchildren we so desperately crave?'

• •

'My dad is waiting until he loses weight before buying new clothes. So he's still wearing his Cub Scout uniform.'

RITA RUDNER

• •

SILLY PRANKS THAT DADS JUST CAN'T RESIST

- **When someone in the family bends over, he makes a loud farting noise.**

- He makes bunny ears behind people in family photos.

- **He pulls funny faces in family photos, even at weddings, much to the dismay of the official photographer.**

- When his wife sits affectionately on his knee, he pretends she is a ventriloquist's dummy.

A Gruesome Prank

One evening when Robbie was five or six, he was sitting in the kitchen with his dad, deciding what to eat. Then his dad started rubbing his eye and complaining that there was something in it. He continued rubbing his eye before, in exasperation, walking over to the cutlery drawer and pulling out a fork. Confused, Robbie asked him what he was doing. His dad looked back, smiled, and replied: 'Don't worry. I just really need to scratch my eye.' He then bent down with his hair covering his eye and made it appear that he was puncturing his eye with the fork, until white gloop began to spurt onto the counter!

Robbie immediately freaked out. He started screaming and running around the house. At one point he ran into the bathroom, looked in the mirror and told himself: 'This isn't happening! This isn't happening!' It was only when he returned to the kitchen and saw his dad in fits of laughter – and still with two good eyes – that he realized he had been well and truly pranked.

Dad had hidden a little mayo packet in his sleeve, and that was what he had secretly placed over his eye and punctured. Robbie says his dad used to play a similar joke on his sister, involving power tools, his leg and tomato ketchup.

- **He secretly tapes his child's phone to the underside of a chair at the kitchen table and then calls it, watching with delight as they go haywire trying to find it.**

- He still plays April Fool's jokes on his children long after they have left school. Even though his eldest son is thirty-eight and one of the country's most eminent urologists, he is not too old, in his dad's eyes, to be handed a piece of paper with the number of the local zoo on it and asking him to call Mr C. Lion.

COMPETITIVE DADS

No matter how much they may try to maintain otherwise, dads are incredibly competitive. Whatever they are playing, be it Scrabble or squash, tiddlywinks or tennis, they always play to win. They never take the age of their opponent into consideration. They are as intent on beating their five-year-old kid at mini golf as they are at beating another dad. They justify the former as being character-building while the latter is viewed as a matter of family honour, like something out of *The Godfather*.

Most dads resist the temptation to humiliate their children too much in the sporting arena. Punching the air and chants of 'Loser, loser!' are actively discouraged. There is little satisfaction to be had from absolutely destroying your child at chess, especially when they are not yet old enough to talk. Instead, dads prefer to go easy at first to make it an even, interesting contest and to give their offspring hope. But if there is even the slightest danger of the child winning, dad will step up the pace to snatch victory right at the end. The child will think that they came close to beating their dad, while he will know that he won with plenty in reserve. Everybody is happy.

Of course, as his children become older, stronger and more confident, dad can no longer always take victory for granted. If he does feel under threat, he can give himself an advantage by making sure that he has access to better equipment, at golf, for example, than his opponent. Restricting his child to the use of a putter and a rusty six-iron while he carries a full bag of brand new clubs is one way of swinging things in his favour. If that fails, the dad can always invoke obscure rules, mostly made up on the spot, to penalize his opponent. Naturally, dad's word is final.

The last resort is cheating. It's not pretty, it's not nice, but sometimes it's necessary. However, there are occasions when, no matter how hard he tries to bend the rules or intimidate, dad just has to accept that he is second best – but don't expect him to be gracious in defeat.

THE WORDS OF A DEFEATED DAD

'It was a close-run thing. Let's call it a draw.'

'Don't get too cocky.'

'It was just your lucky day.'

'It's only a game.'

'Winning or losing doesn't matter. It's the taking part that counts.'

'Best of three?'

'Go to your room.'

• •

'I think the saddest day of my life was when I realized I could beat my dad at most things, and Bart experienced that at the age of four.'

HOMER SIMPSON, *THE SIMPSONS*

• •

MORE DAD JOKES

What happened to the butcher who accidentally backed into his meat grinder?
He got a little behind in his work.

Have you ever tried to eat a clock?
It's very time-consuming.

Why did the scarecrow win an award?
Because he was outstanding in his field.

Did you hear about the explosion at a
cheese factory in France?
There was nothing left but de Brie.

Why can't a nose be twelve inches long?
Because then it would be a foot.

What do you call a bear without any teeth?
A gummy bear.

I'm reading a book on the history of superglue.
I can't put it down.

What time did the man go to the dentist?
Tooth hurt-y.

Why did the picture go to jail?
Because it was framed.

If a child refuses a nap, are they guilty
of resisting a rest?

Who was the roundest knight at King Arthur's Round Table?
Sir Cumference.

I had a neck brace fitted years ago and I've never looked back since.

What did the drummer call his twin daughters?
Anna one, Anna two.

Did you hear the rumour about butter?
Well, I'm not going to spread it.

Did you hear about the Italian chef who died?
He pasta way last week.

What do you call a snowman with a six pack?
An abdominal snowman.

My son kept chewing on live electrical wires,
so I had to ground him.

Why aren't koalas real bears?
They don't meet the koalafications.

Which 15th-century Romanian antelope butchered hundreds of people by skewering them to death with its horns?
Vlad the Impala.

What do you call a man with no nose and no body?
Nobody nose.

WE'RE TALKING ABOUT YOU, DAD

A father is someone who carries pictures where his money used to be.

A father is an ATM in trousers.

Alcohol was my father's answer to everything. He didn't drink; he was just hopeless at quizzes.

My dad wears the trousers in our house – at least after the court order.

One day my boys will wise up and realize they get to stay up playing video games only as long as I'm winning.

I read somewhere that twenty-eight is too old to still live with your parents. It was on a note, in my room.

• •

'From watching my dad, I learned a lesson that still applies to my life today. No matter how difficult a task may seem, if you're not afraid to try it and if you really put your mind to it, you can do it. And when you're done, it will leak.'

DAVE BARRY

• •

A DAD'S GUIDE TO CHILDREN'S PARTIES

One of the most exacting challenges a dad has to face in life is when his home is the setting for a children's party. Indeed, the experience can be so traumatic that many parents now hire special venues for their child's party, where burly security men and guard dogs can be called upon to keep the rampaging five-year-olds in order and to check for illegal substances such as vodka and Play-Doh.

For those who still choose to operate 'in-house', a dad at a children's party is not so much a host, more a referee. He must adjudicate on who was moving when the music stopped during a game of musical statues, and whose bottom occupied the greater part of the last seat in musical chairs, all too aware that his decision could spark a bout of pinching, punching, name-calling and pizza throwing. He must remember that the boy who is lactose intolerant must not be allowed anywhere near the ice cream, and that the girl with agoraphobia is perfectly happy playing alone in the cupboard under the stairs. And all of this goes on while he has to watch his house being systematically wrecked.

Even when he thinks it's all over, his pain is dragged out by those parents who treat the occasion as a crèche and don't arrive to collect their children until two hours *after* the stipulated pickup time. But eventually everyone has gone and the room can slowly return to looking more like a lounge than a war zone. As he once again settles into his favourite chair, he can count the afternoon a success if the only one who has thrown a tantrum is him.

THINGS THAT DADS SAY AT CHILDREN'S PARTIES

'Be careful, those curtains are new, Gareth.'

'The cat doesn't like you doing that, Daniel.'

'Mind the speakers!'

Thanks for That, Dad!

Former Spandau Ballet star and *EastEnders* actor Martin Kemp left his radio presenter son, Roman, red-faced in 2020 by calling his Capital FM breakfast show and recounting embarrassing stories from Roman's childhood live on air for thousands of listeners. 'I'm never going to hear the end of this,' said Roman with admirable foresight. 'I'm going to absolutely hate this, aren't I?'

Martin then proceeded to reveal how Roman used to scream in his high chair for his 'little trees' (broccoli), faked a stomach ache in an upmarket restaurant when he was five because he didn't like the starter, and once sulked for three days after Christmas because Martin had given him a kite as a present. He also recalled how, with Roman only a couple of days old, the family were sitting by a swimming pool in California when a bee circled overhead before eventually landing on Roman's 'little dangly bit. It was only tiny,' continued Martin, piling on the torture, 'I don't even know how the bee saw it!' Powerless to prevent his dad's indiscreet revelations being broadcast to all and sundry, Roman covered his face with his hands in despair while his two co-presenters fell about laughing.

'Yes, Wayne, I'm sure your dad could beat me up but it's still not fair if you win every game.'

'Alice, don't be sick there, you'll ruin the carpet. Do it over Wayne.'

'I need a drink!'

THINGS THAT DADS ARE RARELY ABLE TO DO

- Master emojis. Perhaps it's because emojis are small and a dad's eyesight isn't as sharp as it used to be, but it is all too common for someone to send a sad phone message to their dad and to receive a smiley face in return.

- Refuse the offer of a cooked breakfast.

- Ask for directions. Instead they will say, 'I know it's around here somewhere,' and drive in circles for two hours.

- Multitask, unless you count drinking beer while watching TV.

- Give concise directions to anywhere, even if it's just two streets away. Instead they always have to be long-winded with plenty of diversions and detours. 'Right, what you need to do is turn the car around, take the next turning on the right, opposite the garden with the nice blue hydrangeas – I never know how she gets them that colour – then follow that road round to the right past the house with the Winnebago on the drive and then at the end in about a hundred yards you'll come to a T-junction. If you turn left, it will take you into town past the university and the hospital – it's about two miles, a nice straight road with a bus lane the entire length, so you're never stuck behind a bus – but you don't want to go that way. Instead, turn right and then turn immediately left opposite the house with the green garage. I think he used to be in the army. Or was it his daughter? Or do I mean his granddaughter? Anyway, that's the street you want. Or I suppose, alternatively, come to think of it, you could stay facing the way you are and take the first left and then the first right.'

● Build self-assembly furniture without swearing.

● Keep their opinions to themselves.

● Resist telling everyone which country a car with a foreign licence plate might be from.

● Use abbreviations while texting. Instead, everything has to be written out in full – complete with correct punctuation – which is why it takes many dads far longer to compose a text than it would to write the same words in longhand. It also explains why the recipient often goes off to do something else, such as running a half-marathon, while waiting for a dad's texted reply.

● Grow old gracefully. A lot of dads struggle with the ageing process. Whereas most women effortlessly go with the flow, men do everything they can to resist it and stay young.

This may manifest itself in a 'midlife crisis', symptoms of which include worrying about their thinning hair; comparing themselves physically to other men their age; buying gym memberships; going to rock concerts instead of poetry readings; looking up old girlfriends on Facebook; spending longer in the bathroom each morning than their teenage daughter; and contemplating buying a first-ever motorbike or sports car instead of another second-hand Ford Ka.

- Get excited about TV period dramas. If there are no fast cars and nobody gets shot, it's not worth watching.

- Say 'no' to their daughters.

The Secret Side of Bono

U2 singer Bono is a rock icon to millions but to his actress daughter, Eve Hewson, he could still sometimes be an embarrassing dad. In an interview with the *Belfast Telegraph*, she described how he used to blast music from the Backstreet Boys in his car in traffic while driving her and her siblings to school, and then get out in his dressing gown and dance with his glasses on. 'We were just mortified,' she said. 'But now I think he's a really fun dad. We tease him all the time, but he teases us back, too.'

A DAD'S FAVOURITE SOUNDS

- 'Would you like breakfast in bed?'

- **Someone else vacuuming.**

- A neighbour mowing the lawn (unless it shames him into doing the same).

- **The gentle purring of a cat.**

- The gentle purring of his car engine.

- **'Dad, this is my new boyfriend. He's a millionaire.'**

- 'Dad, this is my new boyfriend. He's a professional footballer.'

- **'Dad, you won't believe this, but I've finally got a job!'**

- 'It's on special offer, sir.'

- **'What would you like to drink?'**

- 'Your dinner's ready.'

- **The sound of silence while he reads the newspaper on a Sunday morning.**

Filmed the Wrong Daughter

Put a video camera in a dad's hand and he becomes overly excited. He immediately wants to film everyone and everything, imagining himself to be the new Spielberg or Zeffirelli. At least that was the excuse given by Georgia Wilde's dad when he went to film her graduation ceremony from the University of the West of England in Bristol. Instead of capturing Georgia in her proudest moment, he filmed the wrong girl – the one ahead of his daughter. Georgia later wrote on Twitter: 'My dad legit filmed the wrong girl going down the aisle at my graduation. Sums up my dad.' When she pointed out his epic fail, he laughed and admitted: 'I got carried away. I was looking at the wrong one.'

TEN THINGS DADS CAN LEARN FROM THEIR CHILDREN

- Cats do not appreciate having their tails pulled.

- The fire department has at least a five-minute response time.

- In a crowded restaurant, a four-year-old's voice is louder than a hundred adults.

- It is rarely a good idea to pour a cup of fruit juice into an electric toaster.

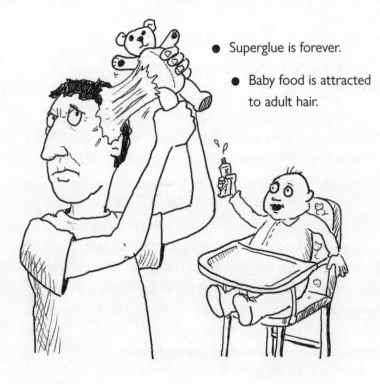

- Superglue is forever.

- Baby food is attracted to adult hair.

- The spin cycle on the washing machine does not make earthworms dizzy.

- Plastic toys do not react well to being microwaved.

- A simple tomato can make a great deal of mess when left in the hands of a three-year-old.

- Just because it has finally gone quiet does not necessarily mean there is nothing to worry about.

School Ban

Celebrity chef Gordon Ramsay was once told to stay away from his fourteen-year-old daughter Tilly's school parents' evenings after he asked the head teacher for a selfie. The next day he received an email from the school saying that he would not be welcome at the next parents' evening. Tilly was so mortified she posted a picture of herself in a T-shirt bearing the slogan: 'Please excuse my embarrassing dad!!!'

'I'm sure wherever my dad is he's looking down on me. He's not dead, just very condescending.'

JACK WHITEHALL

EMBARRASSING THINGS DADS DO AT RESTAURANTS

- He picks up a breadstick and starts to play it like a flute.

- He looks at another table's vegan meal and says it looks like something he nearly stepped in this morning.

- He looks at the chopsticks and says: 'You won't get much knitting done with these!'

- Even though he knows what they are really intended for, he pretends to blow his nose on the Chinese restaurant's hot towel.

- He studies the menu and says: 'Hmmm. Broccoli spears. Is that Britney's brother?'

- He sends back his steak tartare because he says it's not cooked properly.

- He asks you if you are absolutely sure you want your steak rare – even though you are forty-three.

- At the end of the meal he rubs and pats his belly, saying: 'I couldn't eat another thing.'

- He puts all of the complimentary sweets and mints in his pocket – including those intended for everybody else at the table – and says: 'I'll save these for later.'

- When it's time to pay he pretends to have left his credit card at home and says: 'Oh no, we'll all have to do the washing up!'

DADS AND THEIR MONEY

Whereas their grown-up children pay for everything with debit or credit cards, when it comes to smaller transactions dads still like to deal in hard cash. There are few things guaranteed to irritate dads more than queuing patiently at the bar for a beer while the person in front pays for one coffee with a card. By the time the machine has been found, card inserted, PIN remembered, payment accepted and receipt issued, the dad is dying of thirst.

First Date

Jenny was waiting for her new date to arrive at seven. She had talked about little else all day and had made a point of warning her dad to be on his best behaviour. He promised that for once in his life he would be a sensible, respectable parent and would not embarrass her in any way, shape or form. But his tone of mock sincerity meant that somehow she didn't quite believe him.

A couple of minutes before seven, Jenny had a last-minute attack of nerves and made a quick dash to the bathroom. Just then the doorbell rang. Her dad answered it and, barely glancing at the smart young man before him, yelled: 'Clear off, we don't want to be bothered by double glazing salesmen! How many times have I told you people?!' When Jenny came down moments later and heard what had happened she had to run along the street after her date to assure him that it was nothing more than one of her dad's warped jokes. After that they all got along just fine.

It would have been so much quicker with cash. So dads make a point of carrying real money in their wallet for settling things like bar bills, an impulsive banana purchase and taxi fares.

When travelling by taxi many dads feel it necessary to tip the driver out of common courtesy. Exactly why is a mystery. After all, the driver has probably taken the longest route possible, subjected the passengers to his interminable thoughts on what is wrong with the world and charged an exorbitant amount of money for the privilege of listening to him. So to tip him on top of the regular fare is adding salt to the wound. Nevertheless, dads often do it, just as they still tip a barber after a bad haircut. Unless they can see blood oozing from a razor nick or part of their ear is missing, they still deem the haircut worthy of a tip. This explains why dads rarely travel anywhere without carrying a quantity of small denomination coins in their pocket. This also explains why dads rattle and jangle wherever they go, and can be heard approaching from up to fifty yards away.

• • •

'Watching your daughter being collected by her date feels like handing over a million-dollar Stradivarius to a gorilla.'

JIM BISHOP

• • •

WHEN I WAS YOUR AGE . . .

Dads do love to take a trip down memory lane, even if they have to negotiate the roadworks on the A457 to get there. When they finally arrive, it's unrecognizable from the place it used to be, if only because they insist on exaggerating and embellishing the truth so that every little thing about those bygone days turns into a tale of hardship, woe and suffering. By the time a dad has finished with the story, a small patch of flaky paint on his bedroom wall has deteriorated into a swell of chronic rising damp that could have resulted in him catching all manner of deadly diseases from beriberi to rabies. And children will never believe that once upon a time it was necessary to walk all the way across the room to change the TV channel! All this is done by a dad in an attempt to convince his children how tough life was back then, and how they should be grateful for their comparative good fortune today.

And most dads have used a few of the following lines at one time or another to make their point:

'You don't know how lucky you are.'

'When I was a boy, I had to walk twenty miles to and from school every day – often waist-deep in snow – and it was uphill both ways.'

'Schools today are too soft. My school was so tough it had its own coroner.'

'We were grateful to get an orange for Christmas.'

'For Christmas, we'd get a pair of trousers with a hole in the pocket. That way, we'd have something to wear and something to play with.'

'We were so poor that for Christmas dinner we used to go to the nearest KFC and lick other people's fingers.'

'When I was young, we were so poor the ducks used to throw bread to us.'

'We were so poor we used cobwebs for curtains.'

'You don't know you're born.'

'Boredom? When I was your age I didn't know the meaning of the word "boredom". We couldn't afford a dictionary, you see.'

'When I was your age, everyone in the house had to share. I was only able to keep warm in bed at night if it wasn't the dog's turn for the blanket.'

'Our house was so small that half of the TV was in one room and the other half was in another.'

'The house we lived in was so small that the front and back doors were on the same hinge.'

'Our house was so small that if we ordered a large pizza we had to go outside to eat it. But we were happy.'

• •

'House? You were lucky to have a house! We used to live in one room, all hundred and twenty-six of us, no furniture. Half the floor was missing; we were all huddled together in one corner for fear of falling!'

'THE FOUR YORKSHIREMEN' SKETCH,
AT LAST THE 1948 SHOW/MONTY PYTHON

• •

THINGS DADS SAY WHEN ASKED HOW THEY ARE

Most dads are fairly dismissive about their health. So if a casual acquaintance asks them, by way of polite conversation, how they are, rather than give a list of all their aches, pains and ailments, the dads will reply with something non-committal, like:

'Can't complain.'

'Oh, you know, bearing up.'

'Soldiering on.'

'Still above ground. That's the most important thing.'

'They haven't got me yet.'

'Not too bad.'

'Not three bad.'

• • • • • • • • • • • •

'My daughter got me a World's Best Dad
mug. So we know she's sarcastic.'

BOB ODENKIRK

• • • • • • • • • • • •

Has Dad Forgotten Something?

Andrew remembers the occasion when his dad decided to drive the whole family – Andrew, his mum and his baby sister – to the coast for the day. The expedition required lengthy preparation because with a baby there were so many things to remember, but dad was sure he had left nothing to chance. So when he finally sat behind the wheel and was about to start the car he was dismayed to see his wife in the passenger seat looking daggers at him.

'What is it?' he protested. 'I've remembered the baby seat, the nappies, the sanitized bags, two jars of baby food, the baby's bowl, the bottle of baby milk. What IS wrong?'

She said calmly: 'You've forgotten the baby!'

YET MORE DAD JOKES

What do you call a cow with no legs?
Ground beef.

I started a new business making yachts in my attic – the sails are going through the roof.

Did you hear about the new restaurant on the moon?
The food was great, but there was no atmosphere.

Why are soldiers always tired on April the first?
Because they just had a thirty-one-day March.

My son bought me a really cheap thesaurus for my birthday. I couldn't find the words to thank him.

Why is the sky so high?
So that birds don't bump their heads.

What do you call a short-sighted dinosaur?
Doyethinkesaurus.

What do you call a man with a seagull on his head?
Cliff.

What do you call a man with a spade on his head?
Doug.

What do you call a man with three eyes?
Seymour.

**What do you call a woman who is
tied up to a jetty?
Maud.**

What do you call a woman who sounds
like an ambulance?
Nina.

What do you get if you put a duck in a cement mixer?
Quacks in the pavement.

Why did the newspaper blush?
Because it saw the comic strip.

Why was the broom late for work?
He overswept.

What do you get if you cross an eel with a shopper?
A slippery customer.

How do you make a Venetian blind?
Poke his eye out.

Where are dead computer hackers buried?
In decrypt.

Why did the traffic light turn red?
Because it had to change in the middle of the street.

What's brown and sounds like a bell?
Dung.

. . . .

'Austin Powers was born out of trying to celebrate my
father's life. He loved to be silly. When I would bring
friends home to play table hockey in the basement, if my
dad didn't think they were funny, he wouldn't let
them in the house.'

MIKE MYERS

. . . .

Swimming Trunks

To surprise his fifteen-year-old son as he left class on the last day of junior high school in Stillwater, Oklahoma, Justin Beadles ran up to him wearing nothing but tight swimming trunks and a swimming cap, laughing and shouting: 'Jack! Jack!' Poor Jack could not have been more embarrassed as his dad led him away to their waiting vehicle. To add insult to injury, Justin had filmed the whole thing and the video soon went viral. Afterwards, Justin was unrepentant. 'Even if nobody had seen it, I'd do it a million times again because it was so much fun seeing the look on a son who I love, just seeing his face and him looking at me and us knowing deep down inside like, "Dad's an idiot, but he's also kind of OK."'

THE COMEBACK DAD

'Dad, are you going to put the Christmas tree up yourself?'
'No, I was thinking the living room.'

'Dad, I passed Mrs Jenkins in the street.'
'That must have hurt.'

'What's up, Dad?'
'Petrol prices.'

'Hey, Dad, it's nice weather for June.'
'It's nice weather for everyone.'

'Sorry, Dad, I'm running twenty minutes late.'
'Then run faster.'

'Dad, there's something in my eye.'
'Hmmm. Looks like an eyeball.'

'Dad, what's the advantage of living in Switzerland?'
'Well, the flag's a big plus.'

'Dad, do you think I should have given the hairdresser a tip?'
'Yes, you should have suggested that she goes for an eye test before she does anyone else's hair.'

'Dad, could you pick me up?'
'When did you fall over?'

'Dad, how do I look?'
'With your eyes.'

UNSUITABLE SONS-IN-LAW

Dads are very choosy about the sort of person they welcome into the family as a prospective son-in-law. For instance, they may drop strong hints to their daughters that they should not marry or move in with hackers, slackers, shelf stackers, meat packers, writers of jokes in Christmas crackers, magicians, statisticians, dieticians, politicians, polygamists, pessimists, economists,

We Know Where You've Been!

Hannah was thirteen when her dad drove her and her two brothers for a day trip to the beach. On the way they stopped off at McDonald's for lunch. When everyone had finished, her dad told the others to wait by the car while he used the bathroom. He returned to the car park five minutes later, ostentatiously wiping his hands together to let everyone know where he had been . . . and with ten feet of toilet paper hanging down the back of his trousers.

He proceeded to stroll across the car park with a broad grin on his face, milking the attention and calling loudly, 'Hey kids, it's your daddy,' so that even more people would stare at his paper trail. Hannah says: 'Most of them were probably thinking, "Does this guy know he has half a toilet roll dangling from his trousers?" Sadly I knew it was one of his jokes but I still couldn't wait to get in the car and hide. I was so embarrassed by him that day.'

extremists, alarmists, nonconformists, taxidermists, taxi drivers, skydivers, skivers, lifers, snipers, bagpipers, car dealers, card dealers, band members, banned authors, risk takers, undertakers, underwriters, underachievers, drunks, punks, monks, punk monks, hairdressers, window dressers or goths.

A DAD'S GUIDE TO FASHION

If you see a dad wearing something trendy and fashionable, the chances are that it was a present. For despite always wanting to be thought of as cool, dads are a cautious breed, clothes-wise, preferring to stick to the tried and tested rather than risk anything that might make them look ridiculous. Dressing down with the kids is inadvisable when your hair is thinning and your stomach is expanding. Besides, dads are pragmatic. They like to get value for money, so buying something that will be out of fashion in a year's time goes against the grain. Instead they choose clothes that never go out of fashion because they were never in fashion in the first place.

And dads love a bargain. Even if they don't like the design of a particular shirt – sometimes even if it's not in their size – they will still buy it simply because it's in a sale. When mistakes are made, they will insist on wearing the garment from time to time – ideally on days when they do not have to meet their public

– just so that they can say they got their money's worth. This also applies to uncomfortable shoes. Once or twice a year, dads prefer to limp and hobble down the street in a pair of shoes that always pinch their feet to the point of drawing blood, rather than admit that they were a waste of money and throw them out.

In fact, dads hate to throw anything out. A glance in their wardrobe is like travelling back through time. Instead of being put in a charity bag, clothes are relegated to gardening duty, which is why in the 2020s dads of a certain age can be seen doing the gardening in a cheesecloth shirt, flares and platform shoes. It's like watching Elton John dig a herbaceous border. When items become too ragged even for gardening, they are still not thrown out but are hidden away on the top shelf because they may come in useful one day for carrying out a messy household chore. That day never comes.

Family members sometimes try to encourage a dad to spruce up his wardrobe, especially before going away on holiday. He may go so far as entering a shop and looking at a price tag before deciding that his favourite T-shirts have still got another year's wear left in them. You see, it just doesn't pay to be too hasty.

• •

'My dad's trousers kept creeping up on him. By the time he was sixty-five, he was just a pair of pants and a head.'

JEFF ALTMAN

• •

A DAD'S THOUGHTS ON HIS WARDROBE

**'What's wrong with brown? Black makes
me look like a serial killer.'**

'What's wrong with a golf sweater?'

'What's wrong with slippers?'

'What's wrong with wearing trainers with a suit?
They're comfortable, and when you get to my age you'll
appreciate the importance of comfortable shoes.'

'I'll have you know I paid ten quid for that shirt.'

'I like my socks the way I like my coffee: strong, dark
and with a distinctive aroma.'

'What do you mean nobody darns socks anymore?'

'I reckon I can get a few more months out
of those underpants yet.'

'You can't throw that out.'

'It's only one small hole. Nobody will even notice.'

**'These will be all the rage again one day.
Mark my words.'**

A DAD'S THOUGHTS ON HIS KIDS' WARDROBES

'Put some proper clothes on.'

'Why do you need so many shoes? You can only wear one pair at a time.'

'Why pay good money for jeans that already have a hole in them?'

'That's not a skirt, it's a belt.'

'That's almost a dress.'

'Look at the material in that top. It's so flimsy. It will fall apart in a week. In my day things were built to last.'

'What do you mean you've got nothing to wear? You've got a whole wardrobe full of clothes.'

'You almost look presentable.'

'Designer labels are a complete waste of money. You're just paying for the name. You wouldn't catch me in anything with a designer label.'

'You paid how much?!'

• •

'One of the hardest things about being a parent is you're expected to know everything, but you realize you don't because your kids have asked you, "Dad, how does electricity work?" "Er, uh, you put a plug in."'

JACK DEE

• •

AWKWARD QUESTIONS THAT DADS HATE ANSWERING

'Dad, how do you make babies?'

'Dad, when am I going to get a little sister?'

'Dad, why can't I have a puppy?'

'Dad, why can't I paint my room black?'

'Dad, why can't I have a motorbike?'

'Dad, how many girlfriends did you have before you met Mum?'

'Dad, why do Dennis's parents live in a bigger house than us?'

'Dad, why do you eat dead animals?'

'Dad, why haven't you got a job at the moment?'

'Dad, why did you sleep on the
couch last night?'

**'Dad, how can you be in the doghouse when
we don't have a dog? Does that mean
we're going to get one?'**

'Dad, are you losing your hair?'

**'Dad, if x=6, what is the value of y in the equation
xy(y-4) = 28?'**

'Do you know why I pulled you over, sir?'

. . . .

'When I'd fight with my sister in the back seat of the car,
my dad would say: "Right, that's it. Do you want me to
come back there?" I thought that was a fascinating
idea . . . since he was driving.'

BOB STROMBERG

. . . .

Mistaken Identity

When Megan was in ninth grade, one night her friend slept over at her house. The next morning, Megan woke up first and, not wanting to disturb her friend, quietly left the bedroom, got some breakfast and sat in the living room until her friend woke up. However, her dad didn't know there was a guest and neither did he notice Megan in the living room. So, he went into his daughter's room as usual and, seeing someone in bed and thinking it was Megan, rubbed her leg, saying: 'Good morning, sweetie.' It was only then that he realized to his horror that the leg belonged to Megan's friend. Megan says ruefully: 'She screamed and never slept over again after that.'

THINGS DADS SAY ON FAMILY OUTINGS

'We'll take packed lunches. I'm not paying café prices.'

'Let's set off early to beat the rush.'

'Of course we're not there yet. We've only just turned out of our driveway.'

'Why is every idiot out on the road today?'

'Don't shout! I did see him. And I was nowhere near hitting him.'

'Well, you drive if you think you can do better.'

'Can't we find a radio station that plays some decent music?'

'You can't be hungry. You've only just had breakfast.'

'Don't fight in the back. Can't you two just get along for once?!'

'This car is not a playground.'

'I'll turn this car around if you don't behave.'

'I'll leave you at home next time.'

'Can you hold it in for a bit longer?'

'We'll be there in five minutes.'

'You can't be sick. I only cleaned the car last week.'

'We will be there in five minutes.'

'We're not lost. I'm just not sure where we are.'

'We'll be there in FIVE minutes.'

'We're there now, and great, hardly any cars around.'

'How was I meant to know it would be closed?'

● ●

'If you ever want to torture my dad, tie him up and, right in front
of him, refold a road map incorrectly.'

CATHY LADMAN

● ●

Welcome to the World

Jean still remembers how her husband Bill welcomed the arrival
of their first son. Peering into the crib, he said to the baby: 'It
was either you or another cat. Make sure I don't regret this.'

THE DAD DRAWER

Somewhere in the house every dad has his own special drawer
where he keeps an assortment of unrelated objects that he
has never quite got round to throwing out. This is an Aladdin's
Cave of Domestic Minutiae, where items may date back several
decades. The contents of this drawer will almost certainly include
some of the following:

● Odd batteries of all sizes, the majority of which have already
been used and therefore have little life left in them. But if he
ever buys an alarm clock that he only wants to use for half
an hour, he is sure to have a suitable battery for it.

- Half a dozen beer mats that he began collecting in his youth until he got bored with the idea. He still keeps them for sentimental value and in case one day they should become historically relevant.

- A pair of unworn cufflinks still in their box, faithfully kept in the hope that this could be the year that he receives an invitation to Buckingham Palace.

- A pile of yellowing receipts from everything he has bought in shops since 1996. So if he ever tries to exchange the floral shirt he bought on a whim seven years ago, but has only worn twice because the family kept laughing at him, at least he has the receipt.

- Various keys that were once used for opening something but he can no longer remember what.

- Redundant pairs of sunglasses. Every three summers he buys a new pair of sunglasses but keeps the previous pair, even though their lenses are smeared in sun cream.

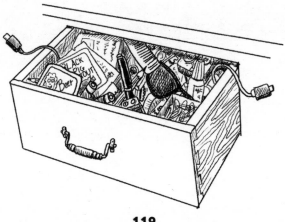

119

- Paper clips and elastic bands of every size and colour because they are sure to be useful for something.

- Miscellaneous leads for electrical appliances that he no longer owns.

- Instruction booklets for those same appliances.

- Pencils from the days before he wrote everything in ballpoint pen.

- A small metal tape measure from a past Christmas cracker, because it could prove invaluable if all the other eight tape measures in the house simultaneously go missing.

- Three bottles of Tipp-Ex even though he hasn't used a typewriter for thirty years. But he keeps them simply because they are still half full and he never throws anything out until it is empty.

- An old comb to remind him of the time when he had enough hair to warrant the use of one. He decides it is worth keeping just in case his hair ever defies medical science and starts to grow again.

. . . .

'My dad was a joker. Whenever I misbehaved, he would bury me in the backyard. Only up to the waist, but you can get real dizzy when all the blood rushes to your head.'

EMO PHILLIPS

. . . .

Cheerleader Support Group

When Corinne Foxx was a cheerleader in high school her Oscar-winning dad, Jamie, decided to surprise her in the most embarrassing way he could think of. He asked her to take a selfie for him and then, without her knowing, had the picture printed onto T-shirts. So at her big game a few days later, he appeared in the stands along with the whole family – about twenty people – all wearing T-shirts with Corinne's face on them. 'He embarrasses me a lot,' she says ruefully, 'and when he does things like that, I just roll my eyes and want it to stop. He's like a big kid.'

DADS AND THEIR CAMERAS

Every dad fancies himself as a budding David Bailey or Richard Avedon. He used to prove it by subjecting his family to three-hour slide shows, which would feature more than twenty near-identical shots of a building that had captured his interest while on holiday in Scotland, along with endless pictures of something that wasn't the Loch Ness Monster. The only light relief came when a stray thumb wandered into frame, or the slide of Great Aunt Eleanor licking an ice-cream cone appeared on the screen upside down so that it looked as if she had been transformed into a clown.

Being of the old school, dads are convinced that the camera on an iPhone is no match for a proper, traditional camera. So when, on a family outing, a handsome pheasant wanders into view and the children take a couple of impressive, instant photos with their phones, dad is busy putting up his tripod, checking the light meter, the focus setting and the shutter speed, only to discover that by the time he is finally ready, the bird has ambled off and is nowhere to be seen.

This attention to detail means that even the most mundane family snap must be treated as if it is to be part of a prestigious exhibition at a national museum. Thus Dad prepares himself behind the camera and issues his instructions: 'Can you step back a pace, Ellen? Woah! Not that far. Are you all right? I didn't realize you were that close to the edge. Sorry. I'll bandage it later. Don't worry, the blood won't show on the photo because Peter will be standing in front of you. Now George, lean to the right a bit and take your hands out of your pockets. At least try to look as if you're enjoying yourself. Amy, don't do that. Have we got a comb for Peter's hair? Right, I think we're almost ready . . .'

It's at this point that Dad realizes there will be one key ingredient missing from the family group photo – himself. So he finds an unsuspecting couple and asks whether they would mind taking a picture. 'No problem,' they say, which is a big mistake because Dad then launches into a ten-minute explanation of how the camera actually works and of the minor adjustments they may need to make before they take the picture. Just as they are about to lose the will to live and are on the point of walking off, young Peter asks them whether they would prefer to use his iPhone. Fifteen seconds later, the family photo is taken. Everyone is happy – except Dad, who grumbles all the way home about a lack of professionalism and patience.

Stunt Driver

Rachel M. says her dad has a favourite trick that he likes to play on her whenever he gives her a lift in the car. As she goes to open the passenger door, he taps his foot on the accelerator just enough to shoot the car forward a little so that she misses the handle. Her worst experience was when she was a teenager and had gone shopping with friends. Her dad arrived to pick her up and twice he did the trick with the accelerator, causing her to miss the handle both times. 'I just stood there looking at him through the glass. He gestured for me to get in. But then he did it again – for a third time – and I fell over! All I could hear was him howling with laughter in the car and my friends joined in. It was so embarrassing.'

EVEN MORE DAD JOKES

What do you call a donkey with three legs?
A wonkey.

Which city increases its population twofold every year?
Dublin.

What do you get if you cross an elephant with a fish?
Swimming trunks.

Did you hear about the hungry clock?
It went back four seconds.

Where do you weigh whales?
At a whale weigh station.

What is Forrest Gump's computer password?
1Forrest1

What do you call the wife of a hippie?
Mississippi.

**What's the difference between roast beef
and pea soup?**
Anybody can roast beef.

Did you hear about the man who jogged backwards last week
and put on five pounds?

**What happened when a blue ship and a red ship
collided in the Pacific Ocean?**
The survivors were marooned.

Why did the golfer wear two pairs of pants?
In case he got a hole in one.

Why are photographers so depressed?
Because they always focus on the negatives.

What is half of infinity?
. . . nity.

Did you hear that a train full of tortoises crashed into a bus
crowded with terrapins?
The local news said it was a turtle disaster.

Why did Captain Kirk go into the ladies toilet?
To boldly go where no man has been before.

Why did the rabbit eat the wedding ring?
He heard it was eighteen carrots.

**Did you hear about the bumper car
operator who got fired from his job?**
He sued his employer for funfair dismissal.

What happened to the wooden car with the
wooden wheels and the wooden engine?
It wooden go!

**What happened to the wooden car with the steel
wheels and the steel engine?**
It steel wooden go!

Which sexual position produces the ugliest children?
Ask your mother.

* *

'For Father's Day we got my dad a T-shirt that says "Do Not
Resuscitate". He wears it whenever Mum takes him to the ballet.'

GREG TAMBLYN

* *

Always the Joker

For comedian Eric Morecambe life was one long performance. He rarely switched off and would turn a simple trip to the shops as a comic routine to entertain the public, often performing a little dance in the street around his Rolls-Royce to the delight of his adoring fans. It was the same on family holidays. His son, Gary, remembers how Portuguese waiters would pour wine for Eric but he would always pick up the empty glass to taste. If there was a red serviette, he would pretend that he had cut his throat and lay down on the table. He couldn't resist playing to an audience.

Bringing girlfriends home was a nightmare for the teenage Gary because Eric was always there lurking in the background, waiting to appear at an inopportune moment. 'It was funny and terrible at the same time,' Gary told the *Guardian*. 'He was just where you didn't want him to be. I remember coming down one evening to answer the door and of course my father got there first. Five girls had turned up to see me – all around seventeen. He was straight there. "Oh look, Gary, two and a half each." I was just dying . . .'

EMBARRASSING THINGS DADS DO IN FRONT OF THEIR KIDS' TEENAGE FRIENDS

- He dresses like them.

- He fists bumps them . . . unsuccessfully.

- He uses street slang like 'totes' and 'adorbs' and abbreviations like 'LOL' and 'OMG' when chatting to them.

- He offers to show them his old navy tattoo because he hears tattoos have become fashionable again.

- He shows off his flossing moves.

- He attempts youthspeak but gets it wrong, using expressions like, 'You sneeze, you lose.'

- He acts as if he is the first person ever to get a new phone.

- He pretends that he knows how to use his new phone.

- He plays them his wacky Crazy Frog phone ringtone – very 2004.

- He confuses 'FaceTime' with 'facepalm'.

- He thinks that if he takes his false teeth out to show them they will find it funny instead of just plain gross.

- He asks them if they want to hear his Hall & Oates Greatest Hits album.

- He criticizes his kids in front of their friends.

- He praises his kids in front of their friends (this is even worse than criticizing).

- He acts like he is really relaxed about his kids going to a three-day music festival whereas in truth he'll be checking the news every hour in case there has been any trouble.

- He says, 'Hashtag cool with it,' when they set off for the music festival.

• •

'I told my father I was punished in school because I didn't know where the Azores were. He told me to remember where I put things in future.'

HENNY YOUNGMAN

• •

FATHERLY ADVICE

Dads are rarely backward at coming forward with advice. So the following may sound all too familiar:

'A little hard work never hurt anyone.'

'You can't be too careful.'

Crazy Dad

Gary Wake was named Teesside's Most Embarrassing Dad in 2013 for a career of buffoonery that began twenty years earlier when he turned up at the maternity unit for the birth of his son, Lee, dressed as a Teenage Mutant Ninja Turtle. His other crimes include regularly dancing in his underwear while singing Prince songs loudly in a falsetto voice, always coming home from a night out with a new hat and trying to move Lee's fourth birthday back a week until he had been paid so that he could afford to buy him a present.

One escapade that didn't work out so well occurred on Lee's fifteenth birthday, when Gary tried to sneak him into a cinema at half price by claiming that he was only fourteen. Unfortunately he had forgotten that the movie had a fifteen certificate. 'That was embarrassing,' admitted Gary. 'I just saw you got in at half price at fourteen. I wasn't thinking. Maybe I am embarrassing to my son. I think as he grows up I grow down. I just like to enjoy myself.'

'Life's not fair. Deal with it. Just accept that some days you're the pigeon, other days you're the statue.'

'Learn to laugh at yourself. You'll never run out of material.'

'You'll soon realize the value of money once you start earning.'

'It's always in the last place you look.'

'Waste not, want not.'

'If you want your partner to pay undivided attention to every word you say, talk in your sleep.'

'Money doesn't buy you happiness.'

'Never test the depth of water with both feet.'

'Worrying is like a rocking chair. It gives you something to do, but it doesn't get you anywhere.'

'When you go away on vacation put one shoe in each suitcase, so if it gets stolen at least they can't wear your shoes.'

'It doesn't pay to be too modest in life. A peacock who sits on his tail is just another turkey.'

'Fill your mouth with food and not with words.'

'Never try to out-stubborn a cat.'

'The best way to double your money is to fold it and put it in your pocket.'

'The only time the world beats a path to your door is when you're in the bathroom.'

'Be true to your teeth and they'll never be false to you.'

**'Never buy a TV in the street from a
man who is out of breath.'**

'If you want to forget all your troubles, buy a pair of tight
shoes.'

**'Always keep your words soft and sweet
– just in case you have to eat them.'**

'Never tell a lie unless it is absolutely convenient.'

**'Live each day as if it were your last.
Someday you'll be right.'**

'The grass may be greener on the other side, but it took a
whole lot of manure to get it that way.'

**'The only place you'll find sympathy is in the
dictionary.'**

'Do what I say, not what I do.'

**'Always look out for number one and be
careful not to step in number two.'**

. . . .

'My dad used to say, "Always fight fire with fire," which is
probably why he got thrown out of the fire brigade.'

HARRY HILL

. . . .

Selfie Dad

Instead of telling daughter Cassie to stop posting sexy selfies on Instagram, forty-eight-year-old Chris Burr Martin, from Washington, D.C., decided to teach her a lesson by recreating the same poses on his own social media page. To make each selfie a near-identical replica of Cassie's, not only did he mimic her poses and expressions, he also drew on her tattoos, wore fake piercings and painted on fake eyebrows. Within a year his comic portraits with receding hairline and bulging belly had earned him 140,000 followers – nearly double that of his daughter.

A DAD'S GUIDE TO DANCING

Dad dancing has become a phenomenon in its own right, chiefly because most dads possess the rhythm of the average bulldozer. As a result dad dancers fall into two categories – those who can't dance and know it, and those who think they can dance but are sadly deluded.

Understandably, the former are always reluctant to set foot on the dance floor. To them it is an area that is about as welcoming as quicksand, a surface on which, incidentally, they would be no less sure-footed. But there are certain times in life when non-dancing dads may find themselves dragged kicking and screaming onto the dance floor. On such occasions their solitary goal is not to draw too much attention to themselves and to get back to the bar as soon as possible. They go through the motions of dancing by shuffling side to side from one foot to the other like a metronome, keeping the same pace whether the music is Perry Como or the Arctic Monkeys. There is no discernible body movement above the ankles, but they tend to grin a lot and chatter inanely in a desperate attempt to make it appear that they are having a good time. In truth, they would rather be undergoing root canal surgery.

Those dads who believe they really can dance are a different matter altogether. Invariably fortified by alcohol at family or work gatherings, the first alarming sign that they are about to hit the dance floor with a vengeance comes with the casting off of the jacket and the loosening of the tie. John Major is about to become John Travolta. Within seconds they are in full cry, throwing shapes with wild abandon, much to the amusement or embarrassment of everyone around them. Sometimes this frenetic display is mercifully short-lived. One minute they can be flailing away to Foo Fighters, the next they find themselves on the floor in the recovery position because someone with medical training thought they were having a seizure. At present there is no known cure for this manic form of dad dancing, although it is thought that a tranquilizer dart aimed at the buttocks could prove effective.

Shake, Shake, Shake Your Booty

Britain's most enthusiastic dad dancers make an annual pilgrimage to the village of Beesands in South Devon for what is almost certainly the highlight of their year – the World Dad Dancing Championship. Dozens of extravagantly attired, demented dads perform their moves – from ill-advised breakdancing to cheesy 1970s grooving – before a panel of five child judges who patrol the dance floor and tap on the shoulder any father who is deemed neither artistic nor embarrassing. When a dad receives the fatal tap, he must retire. After ten minutes, three dads are left. There is then a three-minute dance-off to determine who picks up the coveted trophy – an Action Man figure spray-painted gold.

Conrad Gillespie, a father-of-two who won his second title in 2017, boasts a sizeable repertoire of chaotic limb movements, including the Funky Caterpillar, the Jackhammer, the Confused Swan, the Lawnmower and the Rusty Robot. Describing the secret of his success, he said: 'You need to open your mind, throw away your pride and release the ridiculous rhythmic magic locked inside every dad. In truth, it's no more than I would do at any wedding.'

'When I dance, people think I'm looking for my keys.'
RAY BARONE (RAY ROMANO), *EVERYBODY LOVES RAYMOND*

Please Stop, Dad!

At his fortieth birthday party, British journalist and enthusiastic dad dancer, Harry Wallop, suddenly leaped into action when Ram Jam's 'Black Betty' began to play. He recalled: 'I overexcitedly jumped from a chair to crowd-surf before giving the audience a few uncoordinated gyrations. I saw my eleven-year-old daughter, Celia, beg her mother to make me stop. But if you can't embarrass your kids at your own party, when can you?'

THINGS YOU'LL NEVER HEAR A DAD SAY

'I don't want to look in the toy shop.'

'Your mother and I are going away for the weekend, so you might want to think about throwing a party.'

'I wish we had a smaller TV.'

'This is so much better than the music we had to listen to in our day.'

'Well I never! We're lost. I'll just have to stop and ask for directions.'

'Why haven't you got any tattoos yet?'

'We had it easy when we were kids.'

'Just take your time in the bathroom. OK?'

'We got you that phone for a reason: texting boys.'

**'Don't worry, someone has to finish
bottom of the class.'**

'I can't open this jar. See if Mum can open it.'

'You want to borrow my credit card? No problem.'

'You don't need a job. I make plenty of money
for you to spend.'

**'You're sixteen. You pretty much
know everything now.'**

'I just love it when the kids talk back to me.'

**'Here are the keys to my new car. Go out
and enjoy yourself.'**

'Stay out as late as you want.'

**'Hey, look at your phone when
I'm talking to you.'**

'I don't really fancy doing a barbecue.'

'I know you're thirty-two, but we really don't want you to leave home yet.'

'Your boyfriend has that "up yours" attitude. I like that.'

'Father's Day? Don't worry about that. It's no big deal.'

'Sorry, son. I don't know any good jokes.'

'No, I insist: you have the last potato.'

Too Much Information

Ruth Shaver, from Schellsburg, Pennsylvania, remembered the time when she came downstairs ready to go to a school dance. 'My dad looked at me and said, "Oh, I'm so glad you're wearing pantyhose [tights]." Then he looked at my mother and said, "Although that never stopped us at the dam, dear, did it?" I couldn't believe what he had just said – and my poor boyfriend was standing there with his jaw practically on the floor.'

The Maltese Were Cross

David remembers a vacation in Malta where late one afternoon his dad took everyone off on a 'family walk'. David had been led to believe that it was going to be just a pleasant, casual stroll to explore a nearby, unvisited part of the island, relying very much on his dad's impeccable sense of direction. But two hours later with the light fading fast, his dad finally confessed that they were maybe, just a little bit, generally speaking, taking everything into consideration, lost. To make matters worse, there didn't seem to be any fellow holidaymakers around to ask. Just then a black helicopter appeared in the sky, hovered above the family group, shone its searchlight and a voice boomed through a loudspeaker: 'You are in a military live fire zone!' After everyone scrambled to safety, David's dad vowed it would be the last time he strayed off the beaten track.

'There should be a children's song – if you're happy and you know it, keep it to yourself and let your dad sleep.'

JIM GAFFIGAN

STILL MORE DAD JOKES

How do you stop your mouth from freezing?
Grit your teeth.

Who would have thought Velcro would catch on?

How could you tell that the rabbit was angry?
He was hopping mad.

What's bad-tempered and goes with custard?
Apple grumble.

Why did the farmer plough his field with a steamroller?
Because he wanted to grow mashed potatoes.

**What happened to the cat that ate
a ball of wool?**
She had mittens.

When the wheel was invented, it caused a revolution.

Why was the guitarist nervous?
Because he was always fretting about something.

Why don't cannibals eat clowns?
Because they taste funny.

What happens if you eat yeast and shoe polish?
Every morning you'll rise and shine.

DADS AND THEIR ATTICS

Whenever grown-up children visit, there is a chance that the conversation will turn nostalgic and someone will ask: 'Whatever happened to my old cuddly panda?' At that point the dad will answer solemnly: 'It's in the attic.'

The answer is intended to be final, to convey the impression that the aforementioned panda is now inaccessible, tucked away out of sight, cheek by jowl, with cuddly gorillas, lions, bears, board games, dolls' houses, photo albums, family heirlooms, old tins of paint, wallpaper tables, things that never worked properly and other items that are taken up to the attic in the hope that they will be quietly forgotten. But the look of disappointment on the inquisitor's face is too powerful for dad to resist. He knows there is only one thing for it: he must cast aside his fears, take his life in his hands and go where no man has been for seven months – into the attic.

Seeing the look of apprehension on his face, others will offer to go in his place, but there is no way he could allow that to happen. Ascending those ten steps from base camp to the summit is a challenge for only the most experienced climber if casualties are to be avoided, someone whose nerves are made of the same steel as the ladder itself. It is a job for dad and dad alone. 'I'll do it,' he says nobly, knowing they may be almost the last words he will ever utter, before adding poignantly: 'I may be some time.' And so he disappears from view, with no safety net, helmet or harness, his only concession to his own safety being to request that a sturdy foot be placed on the bottom rung of the ladder.

Up in the darkened attic there is silence, broken only by the occasional rustling. 'Are you all right up there?' a concerned voice will shout. After what seems like an eternity, a faint reply comes. 'Yes, I've found my old school reports. I'd quite forgotten what my English language teacher wrote about me. Still, at least she knew how to spell "disappointing" and "indolent".'

Some while later he announces, 'I'm coming down,' and makes the final descent, covered in cobwebs and bits of fluff but, most importantly, clutching the precious panda. 'Oh no, it's all dusty,' says its former owner, the same person who had demanded the expedition. 'I don't want to touch it.'

Thus the cuddly toy is discarded within a matter of seconds, ready to be taken back up to the attic at the next opportunity. Yet dad feels no bitterness, no regrets, just the satisfaction of a tough mission successfully accomplished.

Costume Change

For 175 days straight from 2010, Dale Price would dress up in a different, outlandish costume each morning to wave goodbye to his sixteen-year-old son Rain as the high-school bus pulled away from their home in American Fork, Utah. It started after Dale waved goodbye on the first day of school and later overheard Rain telling his mother: 'Mum, don't let Dad go out there again.'

To Dale, that was a challenge. So for the next nine months, every school day Dale would appear at the door in a new outfit. If a pirate, Batman or a *Star Wars* storm trooper were not bad enough, it was even worse when he appeared as the Little Mermaid, Kung Fu Panda or the Wicked Witch from *The Wizard of Oz* in front of a bus full of Rain's friends. 'When he did it the first day I was in shock,' said Rain. 'You don't want to see your dad dressing up in a wedding dress, waving at you on the bus.' Over time, however, Rain got used to his crazy dad, admitting that his morning antics 'went from embarrassing to funny'.

Dale simply said: 'I hope this lives with him for the rest of his life.' It's fair to say that it probably will.

SIGNS THAT YOU'RE TURNING INTO YOUR DAD

- You start wearing tartan slippers.

- You put aside a thin piece of wood specifically to be used for stirring paint.

- You wake up and think it's a good day for a bonfire.

- You have your own favourite chair.

- You start watching the weather forecast on TV.

- You park your car right outside the restaurant so that you can keep an eye on it.

- You choose the cheeseboard over dessert.

- When sitting outside at a pub, you pay more attention to the hanging baskets than the beer.

- You become irritated when the neighbourhood kids play on your lawn.

- You can't understand why young people go out in winter without wearing a decent warm coat.

- You watch a celebrity programme on TV and hear yourself saying: 'I've never heard of any of these people.'

- Your morning lie-in at the weekend does not extend beyond 7.45am.

- You repair things instead of buying new replacements.

- Your once concise stories begin to ramble.

- When you find a sweater you like, you buy three.

- Trips to DIY superstores are the highlights of your week.

- You start taking afternoon naps.

- You leave nightclubs early to beat the rush.

- The first part of the newspaper you turn to is not the sports pages but the financial section.

- You don't know any music artists in the current top forty.

- You start silently nodding at people with the same car as you.

- You start talking about a pension scheme.

- Even though icicles are hanging from the windows, you wonder whether it's really necessary to have the central heating on.

- You find his jokes funny.

• •

'If I turn into my parents, I'll either be an alcoholic blonde chasing twenty-one-year-old boys, or I'll wind up like my mother.'

CHANDLER BING (MATTHEW PERRY), *FRIENDS*

• •

Swift Retribution

When singer Taylor Swift was still a teenager her dad, Scott, sometimes used to accompany her on tour, but she was convinced that he deliberately set out to embarrass her in public as much as possible. She recounts how she would return to a hotel lobby after going out for dinner. All was quiet, beautiful and serene until suddenly a voice from nowhere would scream: 'Hey! That's Taylor Swift!' It was her dad. She would then have to plead with him to stop doing that, although she did concede that his jokes occasionally made her giggle.

LITTLE FIBS THAT DADS SOMETIMES TELL THEIR KIDS

'The ice-cream van only plays music when it has sold out of ice creams.'

'They don't sell replacement batteries for your drumming monkey toy.'

'If you keep pulling that face, you'll stay that way.'

'The animals lying at the side of the road are just taking a nap because the road is warm.'

'Eating spinach will make you strong like Popeye.'

'Eating your bread crusts will give you curly hair.'

'We'll leave without you.'

'Every time you touch something in the store, somewhere in the world a kitten dies.'

'The brown M&Ms are only for adults. So you have to leave them for us.'

'The police will come and arrest you if you don't sit still in the car.'

'The brown cows aren't working today, so we only have white milk.'

'It won't hurt, I promise.'

'A penguin lives behind the fridge, and if you leave the fridge door open you'll steal his cold air and make him angry.'

'The sweets next to the supermarket checkout line are not for sale.'

'Every time you lie, a piece of your tongue will fall off.'

'If you bite your nails, you'll get eaten by bears.'

'The dog ate the rest of your cake.'

'All the oil stains in the street are little children who got run over because they refused to hold their daddy's hand while crossing the road.'

'Watching too much TV will give you square eyes.'

'If you eat more than one marshmallow a day, they will expand in your stomach and kill you.'

'There's a tube connecting your bellybutton to your butt, and if you play with your bellybutton too much your butt will fall off.'

'The internet maintenance man turns the whole internet off at eight o'clock every night, which is why that is your bedtime.'

'The sun won't ever rise again if you don't go to sleep.'

'Don't touch that. It'll turn into spiders.'

'By law you're only allowed to speak 5,000 words a month, and once you've used them up you mustn't speak until the next month. You're currently on 4,990 and there are still two days left in this month, so you need to give your tongue a rest.'

'Santa Claus is dead.'

* *

'My father did not like the word "fart". He had a way of getting around the word and would say, "Who whispered?" And we totally accepted the euphemism in our house until one day my granny said: "Come on, David, and whisper in granny's ear."'

DAVE ALLEN

* *

Half Asleep

Yuki Sayeg, from Queensland, Australia, recalls how after the family cat Taffy died, her dad buried it under a tree in their backyard. However, a few nights later her mother went into the garden and discovered to her horror that the dog had dug up the cat's body. So dad was woken from his slumbers and trudged out into the garden in the dark in his pyjamas and army boots to dig a new burial hole. While he was there he decided to discard the towel in which he had originally wrapped the cat and tossed it to one side. Satisfied with his night's work, he returned to bed. The next morning, Yuki's mother saw that in his bleary-eyed state he had tossed the cat to one side and buried the towel!

A DAD'S GUIDE TO GREETING YOUNGER PEOPLE

Greeting young people can be a minefield for dads because there are so many things that can go wrong and cause awkwardness for both parties. Let's start with:

- *The Kiss.* Once a dad has got to know a son's new girlfriend it is perfectly acceptable for him to greet her with a friendly peck on the cheek. This should be a quick, precise motion with no lingering and certainly no slobbering. Coordination is key. If he goes for the left cheek but she offers him the right, there is a serious risk of a clash of noses, so it is advisable for him to wait for a signal from her rather than to dive straight in uninvited. If either of you is the theatrical type, the kiss could even be planted on both cheeks, but this merely doubles the potential for a catastrophe.

- *The High Five.* Dads who wish to make it appear that they are on the same wavelength as young people – or 'down with the kids' in the modern vernacular – may think it cool to high-five them. A well-executed high five, with both parties in perfect unison, can be a rewarding accomplishment for a dad, something to tick off on his bucket list. But get it wrong and he will be the subject of ridicule. For if he raises his arm but his opposite number does not, he is left in that most awkward of poses, the high two and a half. At best, he has an arm dangling aimlessly in mid-air looking for somewhere to land; at worst, his gesture could be interpreted as a Nazi

salute. To avoid this unwelcome scenario, a dad should say the words 'high five' before thrusting forth his arm, thereby giving warning of his intentions.

- *The Fist Bump.* This is the less athletic alternative to the high five, but it is no less excruciating if only one of you decides to take part. If a dad jabs his fist towards an unsuspecting young man who does not respond in kind, the recipient may feel he is about to be punched and press assault charges. The fist bump should also be avoided if one person is wearing a number of rings because what starts out as a simple greeting could end with the other's hand being covered in cuts and bruises.

- *The Hand Shake.* This is where dads are on firmer ground. Except for when Mr Smee first greeted Captain Hook, a good, solid handshake has never let anyone down. However, dads should remember to ease their grip when shaking the more delicate hands of young women for fear of cutting off their circulation. And while a robust handshake may seem appropriate when greeting young men, it should not be of such force that the pumping action risks pulling the arm from the shoulder socket. Nor should it continue for too long. A handshake that lasts for more than twenty seconds will not only leave both parties exhausted, it may be veering dangerously towards petting. In fact, all things considered, perhaps the safest bet is just to nod and say 'hi'.

Dad Goes to School

Brad Howard Sr vowed that if he received another complaint about his seventeen-year-old son Brad Jr's disruptive behaviour from his physics teacher he would go into school and sit with him in class. The boy probably didn't think he meant it but when, two months later, his dad received another email from Rockwell-Heath High School in Texas, he kept his word and went there on his day off to sit next to his overly chatty son during the science lesson.

Dad arrived early and took a seat at his son's desk, then watched as the boy walked into the classroom, laughing and greeting his friends. But then Brad Jr turned around and was horrified to see his dad sitting sternly in his chair with his arms folded. Brad Jr said: 'I didn't even notice him until after I had said hi to all my friends, but I was super shocked.' Dad soon made himself comfortable while the rest of the class revelled in Brad Jr's embarrassment. The unorthodox punishment apparently paid off because Brad Sr never had to go to school again.

. . . .

'My dad's been around the block a time or two. That's about as far as he can go without getting lost.'

MELANIE WHITE

. . . .

THE COMEBACK DAD

**'Dad, I don't want to answer
the door in my nightdress.'**
***'Why do you have a door
in your nightdress?'***

'Dad, did you get a haircut?'
'No, I got them all cut.'

'Dad, what's on the TV?'
'Dust mostly.'

'Dad, how long will dinner be?'
'Four inches. We're having sausages.'

'Dad, can you put my shoes on?'
'No, I don't think they'll fit me.'

'Dad, have you seen my sunglasses?'
'No, son, have you seen my dad glasses?'

'Dad, I'm hungry.'
'Hi, hungry. I'm Dad.'

'Dad, can you put the cat out?'
'I didn't know it was on fire.'

**Dad: 'Son, will you go to the hardware store
and buy me some nails?'**
Son: 'How long do you want them?'
Dad: 'I was rather hoping to keep them.'

● ●

'My father hated radio and could not wait for television to be
invented so he could hate that, too.'

PETER DE VRIES

● ●

He Really Thinks He's Funny!

Whenever the family car drove past a cemetery, Mike's dad
would say: 'Do you know why I can't be buried there?' Even
though they knew what was probably coming, one of the
children would naively ask: 'No, why?' Whereupon his dad
would gleefully exclaim: 'Because I'm not dead yet!'

EMBARRASSING THINGS A DAD DOES AT SCHOOL SPORTS DAYS

- He turns up in full running gear, including spiked shoes.

- He limbers up with a series of squat exercises and press-ups before taking part in the egg and spoon race.

- He stands at the start line with 'We Are the Champions' playing at full blast on his phone.

- He finishes last.

THINGS DADS SAY AND WHAT THEY REALLY MEAN

**'Do you want to go bowling?' MEANS
'I want to go bowling.'**

'I can't believe you're eleven today' MEANS
'I forgot your birthday.'

**'OK, let's clean up as fast as we can' MEANS
'I've just heard your mother's on her way home.'**

'How are you getting on with your homework?' MEANS
'When are you going to start your homework?'

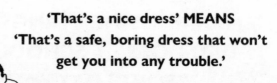

'That's a nice dress' MEANS
'That's a safe, boring dress that won't
get you into any trouble.'

'Who wants beans on toast?' MEANS
'It's the only thing I can cook.'

'Are you eating well?' MEANS
'Are you using the pots
and pans I bought you?'

'How lovely to hear from you!' MEANS
'Why don't you call more often?'

'Was the jacket in a sale?' MEANS
'Surely you didn't pay full price for it!'

'I think I might be going down with something' MEANS
'Leave me alone, please.'

'We're going to watch cartoons now' MEANS
'I'm going to have a doze on the couch.'

'It's nothing. It's only a little ache' MEANS
'I demand some sympathy.'

'Are you still seeing Ryan?' MEANS
'What are you doing still seeing Ryan? Why haven't
you finished with him? He's a waste of space.'

'Did you have a nice time?' MEANS
'Did you pull?'

'What time did you get in last night?' MEANS
'I was looking at the clock at fifteen-minute intervals
from five past eleven and I didn't hear the key in
the door until a quarter to three. What's your
explanation for staying out so late?'

'Are you sure you want to move in with him?' MEANS
'I don't think you should move in with him.'

'Don't feel pressured into getting married' MEANS
'I don't want to pay for a wedding.'

'What are your flatmates like?' MEANS
'Are they all as untidy as you?'

'That's an interesting point of view' MEANS
'You're wrong.'

'Do you think that's a good idea?' MEANS
'That's a really bad idea.'

'Is that the time?' MEANS 'It's time for you to leave.
I want to go to bed.'

When on the phone: 'I'll let you go now' MEANS
'I've run out of things to say. Go away.'

'Have you settled in yet?' MEANS
'When can I come and visit?'

'How about going for a nice walk in the country?' MEANS
'I know a good country pub.'

'You know you can always talk to me if you
have any worries' MEANS
'Except when there's football on TV.'

'You know you can tell me anything' MEANS
'Except for the result of the football on TV.'

'Would you like me to give your car
a quick wash?' MEANS
'It doesn't look as if it's been cleaned since
the day you bought it.'

'Has your lawnmower broken?' MEANS
'Get that lazy husband of yours off his backside.
The grass in your back garden is so long there
could be a herd of zebras hiding in there.'

'Your mother and I were hoping
for an early night' MEANS
'Don't come barging into our bedroom
unless you want to be traumatized
for the rest of your life.'

'What does your mother say?' MEANS
'I don't want to make a decision.'

**'Have you asked your mother?' MEANS
'It doesn't matter what I think. Your mother
has the final word. And I'm scared of her.'**

'Don't tell your mother' MEANS
'Please, please, please don't tell your mother, or I'm toast.'

● ●

'My father makes money the American way.
He trips over stuff and sues people.'

DOMINIC DIERKES

● ●

I CAN'T BELIEVE THERE ARE
MORE DAD JOKES

What did the judge say when the skunk walked
into the courtroom?
'Odour in the court!'

What do you call a sheep with no legs?
A cloud.

Why is it hard for a ghost to tell a lie?
Because you can see right through him.

What wash up on very small beaches?
Microwaves.

What do you call an elephant that doesn't matter?
An irrelephant.

As I suspected, someone has been adding soil to my garden. The plot thickens.

What do you do with dead chemists?
Barium.

What did the grape do when it got stepped on?
It let out a little wine.

Why don't skeletons go to parties?
Because they have no body to go with.

What's black and white and goes round and round?
A penguin in a revolving door.

Why couldn't the pirate play cards?
Because he was sitting on the deck.

How should you deal with an angry, three-hundred-pound baked potato?
Just butter him up.

What do you call a very religious person who sleepwalks?
A roamin' Catholic.

I've just been diagnosed as colour blind. I know, it really came out of the green.

What did the daddy chimney say to the baby chimney?
'You're too young to smoke.'

Why did the admiral decide not to buy a new hat?
He was afraid of cap sizing.

Why is it hard to carry on a conversation with a goat?
Because they're always butting in.

**Did you hear about the man who cut off the
left side of his body?
He's all right now.**

What do you call a can opener that's broken?
A can't opener.

A Bad Report

Ben was worried about showing his dad his school report,
but knew that there was no way he could put it off any
longer. With the incriminating document held tightly behind
his back, he gently broached the subject. 'Dad,' he began,
eyes fixed on the floor, 'sorry, but my grades aren't very
good this term.' Instead of registering annoyance, his dad
simply replied with a lame joke. 'Son, you better get the
snorkel ready if you're going below C level.' It was the one
time in his life that Ben was glad to hear a dad joke, and he
was so relieved he actually laughed.

DAD THE TAXI SERVICE

Dads are forever lamenting the fact that the only time their teenage children want to be seen with them in public is when they are a free taxi service Even then, the rules are clear. Dad must drop them off well away from their friends and without any form of communication, especially affection. He must drive off immediately, not lingering to ensure that they have safely reached their destination. It also goes without saying that he must do nothing to draw attention to himself. This includes driving a make or colour of car that is considered uncool, activating novelty car horns, excessive waving and the wearing of ridiculous headgear.

The best way for a dad to put a stop to being treated as a taxi service is to behave in such an embarrassing manner that his children would rather catch three buses than ever ask him for a lift again. Here are a few handy suggestions for weary dads:

- When dropping your children off, blow loud and demonstrative kisses to them in front of their friends.

- As your children exit the car, call out: 'I hope your haemorrhoids don't hurt you too much when you're sitting down. And we'll sort that big, nasty verruca out when you get home.'

- When giving your children's friends a lift home, play dreadful, cheesy, middle-of-the-road music on the car stereo.

- Sing along to the music.

- Ask intensely personal questions like: 'Did you have a good time?'

- Mention your son/daughter's childhood habits – 'Did you know Jamie used to suck his thumb/wet the bed until he was seven?'

- Wear shorts.

A Teenage Strop

Gregor's teenage son, James, was 'getting gobby' in the car on the way to Scout camp. Gregor eventually dropped him off but as the boy marched away sullenly, Gregor decided to pay him back. As he drove past James and his friends, Gregor threw a teddy bear out of the car window and shouted: 'James, don't forget Ted. You know you can't sleep without him!' His friends were left doubled up with laughter.

DADS AND THEIR SOCKS

A dad can never have too many pairs of socks, which is just as well because that is pretty much what he receives every birthday and Christmas. Father's Day is different: then he usually receives a gift voucher – to buy socks. Maybe because he owns so many pairs, a dad tends to feel naked without socks and is reluctant to walk barefoot even in thirty-degree heat.

And then there is the question of hygiene. Foot care is fairly low on the average dad's to-do list, with the result that his feet can, over time, become gnarled and yellow like a diseased tree stump. Rather than exposing these imperfections to the world by going barefoot in sandals or trainers, he prefers to cover up the offending items with socks.

Dads are generally conservative about their socks, particularly as they get older. Instead of brightly coloured socks that scream, 'Look at me, I'm wacky,' a dad tends to rely on grey, beige or black for winter (or navy blue if he is feeling particularly racy) and white for summer. The uncanny thing about a dad's socks is that they appear to have a life of their own and individual socks can pop up all over the house where least expected – in the bathroom, the cutlery drawer, even the freezer.

A dad can also get very attached to his socks, especially if he tries to put them on while his feet are still wet. So it is a sombre moment when he notices that one has developed a hole or has worn through the heel. Ever the pragmatist, he will not throw out both socks of the pair, but will keep the intact one in the

hope that in a month or two it will be able to forge a lasting union with another newly widowed sock, ideally the same colour. Or he can just wait until his birthday.

Protective Dad

When his eight-year-old daughter, Katie, asked if she could walk to her Knoxville, Tennessee, school alone for the first time, protective dad Chris Early decided to follow her with a drone. He used the device to hover above his daughter and send back live video footage so he could be sure she reached school safely. He explained: 'It was just kind of a thing to keep an eye on her, to make sure she was looking both ways, to let her know that Daddy is always watching.' Although he maintained it was a one-off, it didn't stop *Time* magazine labelling him the 'world's most embarrassing dad'.

SIGNS THAT YOU MAY BE AN OVERPROTECTIVE DAD

- You carry out a full risk assessment before allowing your child to climb onto a small play area slide.

- You buy your three-year-old a plastic pedal car and the first thing you do is fit a seat belt.

- You tell your children that Santa's grotto has been burned to the ground, because you don't want them talking to a stranger.

- It's you, not your children, who insist on checking under their bed at night for the bogeyman.

- You think your child's school uniform should be a suit of armour.

- To stop them falling over and hurting themselves, you would like to carry your children around in a sling until they are at least seven years old.

- Even when they are fifteen, you like to hold their hand when they cross the road.

- You get a job as a school crossing patrol man, just so that you can keep an eye on your children on their way to school.

- Before permitting any of your children to take part in a sleepover at a friend's house, you conduct security checks in the premises and check out the family. To be on the safe side, you also call them every hour through the evening and first thing the next morning.

- You refuse to let your children climb trees, telling them they could be savaged and maimed by woodpeckers.

- You reluctantly agree to buy your child a bicycle, but only on condition that they complete 200 miles of accident-free riding round and round the yard before venturing within one mile of a side road.

You also buy a professional-grade helmet, elbow pads, knee pads and a first aid kit that would be the envy of most hospitals. When they do finally cycle on a public road, you run alongside them on the pavement all the way, carrying a red flag in case you need to stop the traffic.

- When travelling abroad, you make your children spend the entire flight in the brace position.

- You download an app so that you can trace the movements of your son or daughter's phone twenty-four hours a day.

- For years you tell your children that the internet is broken, and when you do finally relent and let them go online you make sure that you choose their email addresses and passwords.

- You make your children sign a written, legally binding contract assuring you that, for the duration of your life, they will never get a tattoo or a body piercing.

- You take a close interest in teenage girls' fashion, steering your daughter towards warm coats, cardigans, long skirts and sensible shoes.

- You think about organizing a search party if your children go five minutes past their curfew time.

- You constantly remind your daughters of the perils of smoking, alcohol, drugs and wearing make-up.

- You hire a private detective to follow your daughter on her first date.

Snap Question

Dads do their best to embrace modern terminology but sometimes they get it horribly wrong. Joanna's dad had worked in a factory for thirty years, so when he dressed in a suit and tie for a special evening out it was such a rare occurrence that he wanted to commemorate the moment for posterity. Handing her the camera, he asked: 'Mind taking a selfie of me?'

A DAD'S GUIDE TO SNORING

If there is one thing at which dads really excel it is falling asleep. Following a hearty lunch, washed down by a glass or two of wine, they can be asleep in a matter of minutes, often coinciding with the very moment that the dishes are ready to be washed. Some dads have even developed the ability to fall asleep mid-sentence. One minute they are happily yapping away about all the potholes in the street or the weather prospects for the next three weeks, the next they are fast asleep, possibly because the subject of their own conversation is so tedious it has induced a state of slumber.

Although watching a baby or a pet sleep can be calming and therapeutic, watching a dad sleep is something different altogether because it is invariably accompanied by snoring. Snoring dads fall into two categories: the light snorer who provides nothing worse

than a diverting backdrop, and the heavy snorer who can cause an entire building to shake.

The light snorer is experiencing a peaceful sleep, the sleep of someone with a clear conscience. For most of the time he wheezes gently, disturbing nobody. If his head flops to one side, a rivulet of drool may seep from his mouth, but there is rarely enough to flood the floor. Also, his body may produce the occasional involuntary twitch to keep dad watchers entertained, but in general there is no cause for alarm. However, this apparent tranquillity can sometimes be rudely interrupted by a sudden loud snort, reminiscent of a hog hunting for truffles. This is most likely caused by the dad experiencing a deeply traumatic dream, such as discovering an odd sock or being unable to find a parking spot at the supermarket.

The heavy snorer is a more formidable beast. Adopting the all-too-familiar pose of head back, mouth wide open, he emits a fearsome sound that can best be compared to a steam train, a pneumatic drill or a rutting stag. He easily drowns out the TV and over time could probably wake the dead. Concerned that he may do himself an injury or at the very least wake up with a seriously dry throat, family members sometimes try to snap him out of it. Those with a mischievous streak may attempt to lob peanuts into the dad's gaping mouth, but this is not recommended as it could cause him to choke. More considerate souls follow a practice known as 'dad whispering'. By quietly repeating 'ssshhh', they can often take the dad several notches down the Richter scale without actually waking him. Akin to hypnotism, it can be a most impressive sight. Of course, when he does finally wake up, he will flatly deny that he has been snoring or even that he was asleep. So it's a good job that someone in the room recorded a video of his loudest blasts on their phone.

• •

'My father never slept like a baby. He slept like a piece of agricultural pumping machinery.'

GRIFF RHYS JONES, *SEMI-DETACHED*

• •

Text Speak

As soon as Chloe received her exam results she messaged her dad excitedly: 'I got an A in Science!' Her dad replied: 'WTF. Well done!' Chloe was puzzled by his turn of phrase and wrote back: 'Dad, what do you think WTF means?' He replied: 'Well That's Fantastic. That's right, isn't it?'

THINGS THAT DADS SAY WERE MUCH BETTER IN THEIR DAY

Household appliances: 'My parents had the same vacuum cleaner for forty years. Things were made properly back then. Now it's all mass-produced, cheap tat that lasts no longer than the guarantee.'

TV: 'We had decent programmes back in my day, but now you have over 200 channels and nothing to watch. It's all repeats or reality TV. I'd rather read a good book.'

Pubs: 'A good pub used to be part of the community, a welcoming place you'd go to meet up with friends. Now it's all trendy bars serving overpriced cocktails and blasting out loud, boom-boom-boom music interspersed with the irritating sound of fruit machines. You can't hear yourself think.'

Neighbours: 'Time was when neighbours were always popping in and out of each other's houses – and not to steal things. Now you don't see your neighbour from one month to the next. Mind you, that's not always a bad thing.'

Cars: 'You used to be able to identify the make of a car by its shape, but now they all look the same. And they're all silver, making them hell to find in a busy car park!'

Football: 'In my day, footballers were real men and they were allowed to tackle each other. Now players fall over as soon as anyone comes near them. They're just a bunch of big softies.'

Music: 'Don't get me started . . .'

Unscheduled Appearance

During the 2020 lockdown, Jessica Lang, a TV reporter for Suncoast News Network in Tampa, Florida, was halfway through recording a piece to camera from the kitchen of her home about the coronavirus pandemic when her father accidentally walked through the door and into the frame. To make matters worse, he was in the process of putting his T-shirt on, meaning that his bare and rather sizeable stomach was totally visible. Jessica later posted: 'Work from home, they said. It'll be fine, *they said.*'

THE COMEBACK DAD

'Dad, did you see that man washing his
car with his son?'
'Why wasn't he using a sponge like
everyone else?'

'Dad, I'm bored. I really need to throw myself into something.'
'Have you tried the pool?'

'Dad, my face hurts.'
'Not as bad as it's hurting me.'

'Dad, I was thinking . . .'
'I thought I could hear something burning.'

'Dad, do you know what?'
'I'm not sure. Does what know me?'

'Dad, put it in my bottom drawer.'
'I didn't know you had a drawer in your bottom.'

'Dad, do you want me to bring up breakfast?'
'No, it will make a mess on the carpet.'

'Dad, it's not your job to embarrass me!'
'I know, but it's one of the perks.'

'I'll call you later.'
'Don't call me later. Call me Dad.'

T-shirt Warning

John remembers how the first time his girlfriend's parents came over for dinner, her dad wore a T-shirt, on the back of which was printed 'Rules For Dating My Daughter'. The rules included: 'Understand I don't like you'; 'If you lie to me, I will find out'; 'She's my princess, not your conquest'; and, ominously, 'I don't mind going back to jail.' Fortunately John knew her dad was only joking . . . or at least, he hoped he was.

'Father's Day, when you get that lethal combination of alcohol and new power tools.'

DAVID LETTERMAN

LOVING MESSAGES IN FATHER'S DAY CARDS

To my favourite ATM.

Your Father's Day gift is another year of not having to pay for my wedding.

LOVING MESSAGES IN FATHER'S DAY CARDS

I smile because you are my father. I laugh because there is nothing you can do about it.

I would go to the ends of the Earth for you, Dad – if you could just see your way to paying for the ticket.

I would give you what you really want on Father's Day, but I can't afford to move out yet.

Thanks for helping me out financially so I can be an independent person and not rely on others.

Happy Father's Day to one of my favourite parents.

I wouldn't trade you for the world. A new bike, yes, but the world, no.

One day I will give you grandchildren who will probably be as annoying to me as I was to you.

I am so lucky to have a dad with such a big heart, high standards and deep pockets.

Thanks, Dad, for not ever really shooting any of my boyfriends.

I love how we don't even need to say out loud that I am your favourite child.

May your troubles be as few as the hairs on your head.

There's nothing I wouldn't do for you, Dad, and I know there's nothing you wouldn't do for me. So that's what we'll continue to do for each other – nothing.

Dad, thanks for being slightly less embarrassing than all the other dads.

A dad like you is hard to find – there are so many pubs you could be in.

You're by far the best dad I could have asked for . . . until you start dancing.

• •

'My dad was a kind of father figure to me.'

ALAN COREN

• •

That's Not Funny, Dad!

When Lauren was in high school, she and her dad stopped at a convenience store to buy some cat food. One of the most handsome, popular senior boys at her school was the cashier. Seizing the opportunity to cause the maximum embarrassment, her dad looked at the cat food and said: 'Now Lauren, don't eat all this in the car!' Then he walked out and left her standing there, red-faced.

DADS AND THEIR LAWNS

When it comes to gardening, the two areas in which dads take particular pride are vegetables and the lawn. They are quite happy to let someone else take responsibility for any flowers in the garden, but they consider growing vegetables to be very much a man thing, a symbol of masculinity. So the same dad that usually complains bitterly if he has to get up in the morning much before eight o'clock will happily creep out to the greenhouse with a torch, before it is even daylight, just to check that his prized cucumber/ onion/cabbage has suffered no overnight mishap, and is still on course to be the biggest he or anyone else in the neighbourhood has ever produced. It has even been known for a dad to spend weeks nurturing an individual beetroot 24/7, lavishing more care and attention on it than he ever did on his own children, though nobody in the family – himself included – actually likes beetroot. If there is a competition involved, albeit an informal one among friends, to a dad that is a competition to be won. At any cost.

It is a similar story with lawns. When children are young, most dads reluctantly accept that the lawn is a play area for games of football, badminton or just mayhem. However, when the children finally leave home, dads often experience a fanatical desire to create the most immaculately manicured lawn within ninety miles. If they see anyone with a better patch of grass, they are stricken with a condition known as Lawn Envy. The only cure

is to achieve the lawn of their dreams, which requires constant supervision and cutting the grass every single day

Perfect lawnmower lines are the ultimate goal. Worm casts and snail trails will not be tolerated, and any weed that has the temerity to appear will be swiftly and mercilessly despatched. A lawn weed that does escape attention long enough to bloom is likely to give him nightmares for weeks.

And it goes without saying that grandchildren are not permitted to play – or even set foot – on the sacred turf. Instead they are hurried off to the park or confined to a separate, designated area of the garden, such as a hard, unforgiving concrete patio where any fall will be a lesson remembered. The ideal Father's Day gift for the lawn-obsessed dad is therefore one of two signs: 'Keep Off the Grass' or 'No Ball Games'.

• •

'The only person who could start our lawnmower was my father, and he could do this only by wrapping rope around the starter thing and yanking it for a weekend, requiring more time and energy than if he'd cut the entire lawn with his teeth.'

DAVE BARRY

• •

The School Dance

Chicago's Emily Gallagher was distinctly apprehensive when her parents volunteered to chaperone her at her eighth grade school dance – and, as it turned out, with good reason. Her dad had always complained about her listening to loud music so she might have expected him to take precautions against the noise, but even she was horrified when they arrived at the dance. She glanced over and saw her dad put on the biggest set of headphones she had ever seen. She said he looked as if he was standing on the tarmac waving an airplane in. 'And of course the kids around me are going, "Whose dad is that?" And I'm like, "Yeah, whose dad is that?"'

• •

'Fathers are biological necessities but social accidents.'

MARGARET MEAD

• •

NO, PLEASE, NOT MORE DAD JOKES!

What is small, red and whispers?
A hoarse radish.

Why did the policeman stay in bed all day?
He was an undercover officer.

What did the judge say to the dentist?
'Do you swear to pull the tooth, the whole tooth, and nothing but the tooth?'

**Children certainly brighten up a home –
they never turn the lights off.**

What is harder than a diamond?
Paying for it.

**What's green, red and yellow and wears
boxing gloves?**
Fruit punch.

What happened to the guy who went to a seafood disco?
He pulled a mussel.

How do you communicate with a fish?
Drop it a line.

The family that sticks together should bathe more often.

How do you join the police?
Handcuff them together.

Why did the robber take a shower?
Because he wanted to make a clean getaway.

What kind of cheese would you hide a horse in?
Mascarpone.

Did you hear about the dog that ate nothing but garlic?
His bark was much worse than his bite.

I just swallowed some Scrabble tiles. I'm not looking forward to my next vowel movement.

Why did the boy tiptoe past the medicine cabinet?
He didn't want to wake the sleeping pills.

How did the pig feel when he lost his voice?
He was disgruntled.

How do we know that chimpanzees are underpaid?
Because they work for peanuts.

Which pirate drools continuously?
Long John Saliva.

Why did the horse cross the road?
To reach his neigggggghhhhhbourhood.

Pride Before a Fall

When fifty-six-year-old Paul Hunt, from Fife in Scotland, bought a new luxury white BMW i8 sports car, he couldn't wait to show it off to family and neighbours. Unfortunately, the wannabe James Bond ended up looking more like Mr Bean when, after posing proudly behind the wheel, he realized that getting out of the car was easier said than done. Having opened the gull-wing doors, he became wedged between the seat and the steering wheel, and was only able to extricate himself by performing an awkward half twist on his hands. In fact, he made such a mess of climbing out of the sleek, low vehicle that he ended up on all fours in a heap at the roadside, like a dog at a fire hydrant. Uploading the video of her dad's ignominious exit onto social media, his daughter, Ciara, playfully described him as 'the biggest idiot I know'. The video prompted one Twitter user to remark: 'Imagine getting pulled over and the cop asks you to get out and take a breathalyser, and this is how you exit the car.'

A DAD'S GUIDE TO COOKING

Although many of the world's top chefs are men, it is fair to say that there are a number of dads whose expertise in the kitchen extends little further than beans on toast or microwaving a ready meal. His definition of a successfully prepared meal is one where he has not had to call out the fire brigade.

Part of the reason why dads often struggle in the kitchen is because they have so many things to juggle in life – work, the kids, TV, the pub, trying to look busy around the house. Also, although he may have cooked a mean spag bol or paella in his youth, over the years his role in the kitchen has often been reduced to that of supporting artist, performing tasks like opening the wine or loading the dishwasher while his partner takes centre stage with the actual cooking. And they are probably so accomplished that his confidence has taken a knock. His pride has been lightly battered. But transfer the kitchen outdoors and it's a different story. The apprehensive assistant is King of the Barbecue.

The barbecue is very much dad's world and his skill at getting it to light first time ranks as one of his finest achievements, along with making a well-received best man's speech and his school certificate for the fifty metres breaststroke. After cramming the majority of a cow onto the grill in one form or another (thereby quadrupling his family's weekly meat intake in a single session), he constantly turns, tweaks and fiddles with the food in his quest for that charred heaven, beer in one hand, tongs in the other, like an artist putting the finishing touches to a masterpiece. If there was an aftershave that captured the smell of burning charcoal, he would wear it every day. And when his work is done and the last burger has disappeared, he quietly reverts to his role of humble kitchen assistant until the next sunny day.

Party Pooper

One afternoon, Sienna had invited a few of her friends around to hang out in the back garden of her house. They were chatting away as teenage girls do, but her dad was growing bored and restless, always a dangerous sign. So, deciding to spice things up a little, he went indoors and smeared a big scoop of peanut butter on the heel of his trainers. He then walked over to the girls and, glancing down, said: 'What the hell is that on my shoe?! Is that dog poop?' He then sniffed it, licked it and shrieked: 'Ewww! It is dog poop!' All of her friends immediately freaked out while Sienna was left mortified. Dad strikes again!

DAD'S FAVOURITE ARMCHAIR

An orderly family home will have its own set of unwritten rules. These will include not wearing muddy shoes on the carpets, not leaving wet towels on the bathroom floor, not leaving the lid off the cookie jar and, perhaps the one carrying the most serious penalties for violation, not sitting in the dad's favourite armchair.

Dad's chosen armchair is effectively his

throne — especially if that throne has sweat marks from the back of the king's head, a red wine stain on one arm and half a dozen errant dry roasted peanuts lodged down the side of the cushion. Dad's armchair could be old or new, it could be fabric or leather, it could be reclining or upright, but the common denominator is a commanding, regal position from where he can best survey all of his kingdom and, more importantly, the TV. It is also a safe haven where he can relax, feel comfortable, stretch out and, in the blink of an eye, fall asleep.

The chair is such a key part of a dad's life that woe betide anyone — family member or visitor — who attempts to sit in it. To sit in his chair would be like trying on his best shirt or running off with his wife. Even the cat knows better than to curl up on dad's chair. Interlopers are liable to be subjected to anything ranging from a hard stare to downright hostility. When dad is not around, the chair must still be kept vacant, even if it means Mrs Watkins from next door having to perch on a high, hard, unforgiving wooden barstool while her husband sits on the low, wicker laundry basket that leaves deep lines on his backside for days to come so that he looks like a road map of Northamptonshire. This may sound extreme, but any hardship is perceived as worthwhile to ensure the sanctity of dad's favourite armchair before he next lowers his ample posterior onto it.

HOW EMBARRASSING IS YOUR DAD?

1. Does your dad view school parents' evening as . . .

a) An opportunity to have a serious discussion about your progress with your teacher?

b) An opportunity to test his jokes on a new audience?

2. The first time he is introduced to the latest love of your life, is your dad most likely to . . .

a) Keep a low profile so as not to appear overbearing?

b) Crack a few lame jokes to your new partner before discreetly retiring?

c) Dust down the albums containing photos of you when you were young, and make comments like, 'Were you wearing that dress for a bet?' or 'Look at that hair! Who cut that? The butcher?'

3. If a car backfires loudly outside your house, does your dad . . .

a) Ignore it?

b) Say: 'That doesn't sound too healthy'?

c) Collapse to the floor, theatrically clutching his chest and gasping: 'I think I've been shot!'?

4. If your dad is placed in charge of the shopping cart on one of his rare trips to the supermarket, does he . . .

a) Push it around sensibly, waiting patiently to pick up the items on the list?

b) Pretend that he's Lewis Hamilton, accelerating past the old lady who is making a pit stop at the bananas, looking for the apex on the corner exiting the perishable goods aisle and treating the turn from the freezer section into biscuits and confectionery as if it were a high-speed chicane?

5. If your dad hears a large dog barking at him in the street from behind a fence, is he most likely to . . .

a) Hurry on past?

b) Tell it to be quiet?

c) Bark back at it, thereby sending it into a barking frenzy and, in a chain reaction, setting off every other dog in the neighbourhood?

6. Which of these have you ever done or felt like doing?

a) Apologized to strangers for your dad's silliness.

b) Disowned him in public by telling strangers that he's not your dad at all, just some random oddball who keeps talking to you.

c) Double-checked your birth certificate in the hope of finding that you were really adopted.

7. Which of the following has happened while playing football with your dad in the garden?

a) You had to go to your next-door neighbour and ask for your ball back because your dad, in the delusion that he was David Beckham, kicked it over the fence and into their garden.

b) Someone in the family has ended up in Accident and Emergency because your dad became overexcited with his tackling.

c) Your dad has insisted on continuing the game until he was on the winning team, even if it meant playing past midnight.

8. On the beach did your dad used to . . .

a) Build sandcastles with you?

b) Bury you up to the neck in sand?

c) Bury himself up to the neck in sand?

9. Which of these have you ever seen your dad wearing?

a) A baseball cap.

b) A baseball cap worn backwards.

c) Cargo pants (when not on military manoeuvres).

d) Speedos.

e) A hoodie.

f) Trainers with lights.

g) Leather trousers.

10. Which of these has your dad ever done?

a) Jumped in a swimming pool fully clothed.

b) Ridden a child's bicycle along the street.

c) Flirted with mannequins in a department store.

d) Worn a woman's wig in public.

e) Danced a waltz in the street with a total stranger.

f) Accidentally set fire to his hair.

g) Deliberately put all his clothes on back to front.

h) Pretended that he was a chicken for a whole day.

11. At your school fair, would your dad most likely volunteer to . . .

a)   Adjudicate at the 'guess the weight of the cake' competition?

b)   Run the tombola stall?

c)   Stand in the stocks to have wet sponges thrown at his face?

12. Is your dad's favourite day of the year . . .

a)   His birthday?

b)   Christmas Day?

c)   April Fool's Day?

13. Would you describe your dad's signature dance move as . . .

a)   The Self-Conscious Shuffle?

b)   The Arthritic Moonwalk?

c)   The Strutting Rooster?

14. At a fancy dress party which of these character costumes would best suit your dad's personality?

a)   Superman.

b)   The Incredible Hulk.

c)   Fred Flintstone.

d)   Pinocchio.

e)   Mickey Mouse.

f)   Pumbaa.

g)   The Grinch.

h)   Elmer Fudd.

i)   Dick Dastardly.

j)   Goofy.

15. Does your dad ever discuss his and your mother's sex life . . .

a)   In front of you?
b)   In front of house guests?
c)   In front of the rest of the congregation?

Award points as follows:

1. a) 0, b) 2
2. a) 0, b) 1, c) 2
3. a) 0, b) 0, c) 2
4. a) 0, b) 2
5. a) 0, b) 0, c) 2
6. 1 point for each
7. 1 point for each
8. a) 0, b) 1, c) 2
9. 1 point for each
10. 1 point for each
11. a) 0, b) 1, c) 2
12. a) 0, b) 0, c) 2
13. a) 1, b) 2, c) 3
14. a) 1, b) 2, c) 3, d) 4, e) 5, f) 6, g) 7, h) 8, i) 9, j) 10
15. a) 2, b) 2, c) 3

Scores:

1–15: Think yourself lucky – your dad isn't too embarrassing. You don't need to hide him away in the attic when friends visit . . . yet.

16–30: Your dad is just about bearable – but if he gets any more embarrassing, either you or he may need to move out. Give your mother the casting vote.

31–50: Sadly, your dad is certifiably embarrassing. Counselling for you or a straitjacket for him may be your only options.